Human Spirit Rediscovery

BY

ROBERT MILLARD HILL

HUMAN SPIRIT REDISCOVERY

Copyright © 2005 by Judith A. Hill

All rights reserved.

No part of this book may be reproduced or transmitted in any form or by any means, electronic or mechanical, including photocopying or recording, or by any information storage or retrieval system, without written permission from the author and publisher. Requests may be e-mailed to: stelliumpress@aol.com

ISBN 1-883376-14-9

STELLIUM PRESS
P.O. Box 86512
Portland, OR 97286-0512

TABLE OF CONTENTS

BOOK ONE - *THE HUMAN SPIRIT*

	Page
A BASIC BIAS	1
MY GHOST	3
NATURE OF PROOF	5
IDENTIFICATION	7
THE PROBLEM	9
TRUE VALUE	11
WHAT IS A SPIRIT?	15
OUR BELOVED PET	19
THE NEW AGE	21
MAGIC WORDS	23
QUESTIONS AND ANSWERS	25

Table of Contents, Page Two

BOOK TWO - *HUMAN SPIRIT REDISCOVERY*

	Page
PREFACE	33

Part One

THE OUTLINE	37
TERMINOLOGY	39
ORIGIN	43
THE HOMO SAPIENS	45
HOMO SPIRITUS	47
ANIMALIZATION	49
CHART	50
THE CORRECTION	53
LIFE MASTERY	55

Part Two

THE PROGRAM	57
SAPERE SPIRITUS	59
REINCARNATION	61
RESONANCE	63
PEACE	65
BEAUTY	67
TRUTH	69
COMPASSION	71
SUMMARY	73
QUESTIONS	75

Table of Contents, Page Three

BOOK THREE -
SELF AND BASIC ENERGY

	Page
PREFACE	95
INFINITY	97
PLANES	99
INDIVIDUATION	101
VARIETY	103
THE REAL SELF	105
PERSONALITY	107
A WORLD PATHOLOGY	109
SELF...TRUE AND FALSE	113
THEORIES	115
HARMONICS	117
GOLDEN LIGHT	119
QUESTIONS AND ANSWERS	121
CONCLUSION	131

Table of Contents, Page Four

BOOK FOUR -
A GOLDEN LIGHT TEXTBOOK

Part One   *Page*

DEFINITIONS   D1, D2, D3

INTRODUCTION..133

LIGHT EMISSION...135

LIGHT IS ENERGY..137

AUTOMATIC IMPROVEMENT..139

THE ALLY..141

THE SPECTROSCOPE..143

THOUGHT-FORMS..145

THE GOLDEN LIGHT POOL...147

THE AURA...149

ILLUSTRATION   -A-

23'rd PSALM...151

PERSONAL THOUGHT -FORMS..153

Part Two

A WAY OF LIFE...155

BEGINNING MIND SEPARATION..157

(The Golden Light Textbook page numbers are continued
on the next page.)

Table of Contents, Page Five

BOOK FOUR - *CONTINUED*

<u>Page</u>

INTENSE LISTENING	159
SEPARATION MANDATORY	161
SYMBIOSIS	163
CHEATING YOURSELF	165
WHY SEPARATION?	167
OTHER MEANS OF SEPARATION	169

<u>Part Three</u>

A GOLDEN PERSON IS ENLIGHTENED	171
PURIFICATION	173
PEACE	175
CORRECTION	177
FOUR MAGIC WORDS	179
BEAUTY	181
ABSTRACTIONS	183
TRUTH	185
TRUTH REVIEW	187
COMPASSION	189
SUMMARY	191

<u>Part Four</u>

BASIC ENERGY	193
MIND	195
BENEFITS	197
RELIGION	199
THE WORLD	201

BOOK ONE

The Human Spirit

A BASIC BIAS

In writing about the human spirit, the first thought must be : does it really exist ?

Or -   is the concept a delusion ?

As for me, my bias is that I think each of us is a spirit.
And, we "reside" in a physical body.

A further part of my bias, is that each human spirit is a self-aware entity. Also, each physical body is a self-aware entity.

In other words, the spirit does not animate the physical body, as is so often supposed.

The evidence for my bias is of two natures.
First, I honor the enormous amount of collected testimony about the "out of body" experience. And secondly, there is the testimony about the phenomenon called reincarnation. That testimony also seems to validate the existence of a human spirit.

My personal experience with the human spirit contains an interesting event, in which a friend and I had a very close encounter with a ghost.
This will be related in the next chapter.

MY GHOST

Is the concept of a human spirit only a self-comforting delusion ?

I think not. And one piece of evidence I have, to think the spirit is real, is my experience with a ghost.

A description of this event follows.

My friend Al and I were walking, about 2 p.m. We were in a large field, which was about four miles square, so that as we were nearly in the center, we could see two miles each direction.

The field was quite bare, with only a few trees and sparse brush. No one could hide or conceal himself.

As Al and I walked, a man suddenly appeared. We had not seen him appear. He was small, only about five feet in height. He was dressed in an ordinary brown business suit (I did not notice if he wore a tie). On his head was a brown, dusty fedora, very wrinkled. In his hand he had a folded newspaper, which looked yellowed from age.

The man approached, walked by us. He appeared to be a solid and real person, not a figment of imagination.

As the man passed us, he was very close, only about two feet from Al and myself.

As the man passed by, he did not raise his head, which was bowed toward the ground. He did not seem to notice us.

In a few moments, after the man had passed us, Al and I turned to take another look. The man had disappeared !

Al and I were astonished. I immediately thought I could have been hallucinating. So, I asked Al what he had seen.

Al described the man, and his description tallied exactly with what I had seen. This was no hallucination.

Our interest caused us to look about the ground, which was dusty, for the man's footprints. We found none.

To this day, many years later, I am convinced that Al and I saw what is called a ghost.

The experience Al and I had, can certainly be interpreted as something other than our seeing a ghost.

But on the other hand, I don't see how it could be called an hallucination. Two people don't have the same hallucination at the same time.

The man who disappeared, was not flesh and blood. What was he?

My future chapters of this book will give what I hope are reasonable explanations for what Al and I saw.

NATURE OF PROOF

Al and I saw a ghost. In my mind, that is a reasonable explanation of our experience.

And what is a ghost?

According to Webster's dictionary, a ghost is a spirit, which may appear as a semblance of a person; or the ghost may appear as a shadowy form of some kind.

The nature of our thoughts here, brings us to a question; how do we prove <u>anything</u>?

And - how can we prove the human spirit exists?

Our answer is that proof takes three forms: it is scientific, or it is empiric, or it can be testimonial.

Scientific proof is made by repeated demonstrations. Do something again and again, and if results remain the same, a claim is thereby considered valid.

Empiric evidence does not actually prove something. It is instead, a method or belief, practised for so long a time, that its validity becomes taken for granted.

Usually, empiric proof works favorably for us, but once in a while a discovery upsets an established method or belief. Then we have to abandon that particular empiric data.

The third form of proof is by competent testimony.

Proof by testimony demands that it be given by a trusted and competent observer. This type of proof is accepted in a court of law.

However, caution must be taken against "hearsay" evidence, which is not accepted in the court.

To date, no scientific proof of a spirit has been undertaken.

We do have a huge amount of both empiric and testimonial proof.

The empiric and testimonial proof we have is reliable, inasmuch as thousands of trustworthy persons have been involved.

I believe a careful person can accept the bodies of empiric and testimonial evidence for existence of the human spirit.

In the future, one hopes scientists will find the human spirit a subject worthy of their testing.

In regard to testimonial evidence, I recommend the following book by Raymond A. Moody, Jr., M.D. The book is "Life After Life".

Moody's book deals with reincarnation, and he pretty well establishes reincarnation as a fact. And, it is a fact which illuminates the existence of the human spirit.

IDENTIFICATION

If we accept reincarnation as a fact of life, this means the human spirit survives the death of its physical body, in which the spirit had been in residence. The spirit continues to live, but the body ceases.

The spirit is a reality.
We need to question, why is it we have no direct and sensible awareness of the human spirit ?
There is indirect evidence, as provided by Dr. Moody and his book, but there is no directly obvious and clear presence of the spirit.
There is no demonstrable presence.

The human spirit is an important element of our life, and yet it remains an unknown.

My explanation of this odd phenomenon — is that the human spirit <u>believes itself to be the physical body.</u>

The spirit has this belief, because it is so deeply meshed and bonded into and with the physical body.
This belief is a serious mistake made by the human spirit.
All of which explains why no demonstrable presence of the spirit is sensed or seen.

This problem is a sad one, because the human spirit is our real self. We humans are not the physical body. The body is an entity in its own right . . . but it is not us.
These statements are radical, and extremely contrary to the normal feelings and beliefs.

My reader may well ask, "Why does the human spirit's belief it is the physical body - cause the spirit to be silent, and never to express itself ?"

There are two answers to this question.

The first answer - because the spirit feels it is the body, the spirit therefore expresses itself as if it were the body.

At times, you may be hearing the spirit speaking, but it will sound as if the body personality is speaking.

The spirit's beliefs and feelings are so like those of the body personality, that you think the body is speaking.

The second answer - the spirit is usually content to let the body personality speak and rule in all matters.

When the body speaks and makes decisions, the spirit thinks that it is doing so.

There is a perfect unanimity between body and spirit.

I hope this explanation answers the question above. The problem of why we never experience the spirit (and do not know ourselves), is a very dense thicket to get through.

THE PROBLEM

Our problem about the human spirit is that we can't find it.

The only thing we find is the physical body's personality, which is called our mind and its various levels and functions.

My theory is that the body's personality, and the spirit's personality, are so much in agreement, so closely joined, that they appear to be one and the same thing.

Body and spirit, however, are two entities, not one.

We need to find a technique that will expose the spirit as a separate entity. And the technique, of necessity, has to use the physical body's clever mind.

We can't use the spirit to solve our problem. That is because the spirit _is_ the problem.

Using my clever mind (sometimes not so clever), I think we can find a solution by using the same technique employed to bring a person out of a state of withdrawal.

Often, such persons withdraw into themselves, because they have had a severe trauma. They feel it is unsafe to communicate.

The human spirit has not suffered a severe trauma, but it _appears_ to be withdrawn. The appearance is explained on page 8.

Our technique, then, will be the same one used to encourage a withdrawn person, so that such person will resume normal communications.

This technique is common, and is as follows.

The technique used to bring the spirit mind forth, so that it will express itself openly, has but three parts.

(1) <u>Give praise</u> . . . give praise to the spirit mind/personality.

(2) <u>Ask questions</u> . . . ask the spirit to answer questions.
Listen for answers, which may at first be indistinct.

(3) <u>Have high expectations</u> . . . maintain expectation that the spirit personality will express itself freely, and in its own voice.

The expectation implies that the spirit is not the body, and that each entity is entitled to speak for itself.

* * * *

The above technique uses one's normal mind, which we use every day. I call this mind, the physical body mind.

To perform the above technique, you speak to your spirit, as if you are talking to a person. You can talk out loud if you want, but generally, I prefer to <u>think</u> my thoughts of praise, etc., to my spirit.

After practising the technique for a time (the amount of time will vary from person to person) - you will notice a response, deep in your mind. That is the spirit, making itself known. The response will become stronger, the more the technique is practised. You are talking to a real entity, which in actuality is your true self.

Requirements are simple, for this technique. They are time and great patience.

TRUE VALUE

What is the point of getting in touch with your real self, your spirit self ? Is there any reason to do that ?

There are good reasons. Let me give four, to show that getting in touch has true value.

These four reasons are : (1) you acquire access to a huge fund of practical information. (2) You acquire another area of sensation, which has not been used by you. (3) You gain another mind, to assist you in making decisions. (4) You acquire a new way to balance and affect the power of physical instincts.

Following, is a more lengthy explanation of the above four reasons.

<u>A huge fund of practical information</u> . . .

the human spirit has lived many lives, successively, in one physical body after another. Each life gave the spirit various experiences. This is a massive fund of information, which can be useful in practical ways.

The information can be used to make better decisions, than if one did not have such information.

A freed spirit mind makes it possible to get at this fund. If the spirit is not freed, we have little or no access to the fund.

Obviously, being in touch with your true self, has enormous practical value.

<u>You acquire another area of sensation</u> . . .

the term "area of sensation", means that each of our areas of sensation has its own frequencies. All sensation is a sending and receiving of energy waves, which pulsate at given frequencies.

The sensation of sight, for instance, has its own set of frequencies. The same is true for all areas of sensation.

When the spirit becomes free to express itself, it also evidences some sense skills which the physical body does not have.

When our spirit is able to send and receive sensations, in ways the physical body cannot do, we have gained something valuable.

In order to understand how this takes place, we have to recognize that the spirit has its own body, mind, and personality. Its body and mind give it sense skills which are unique to the world of the spirit.

You gain another mind . . .

a spirit mind which is able to express itself (is free), can offer us opinions, and even give commands.

In effect, you then have two minds, and as the saying goes, "Two heads are better then one."

Before the spirit became independent, it echoed the mind of the physical body. (See page 8).

It would be better for humanity if we did not continue to be in thrall to the physical body's mind. This opinion is related to human history, which is not a pretty story.

I believe it very probable that a free spirit mind will remedy the negativism of the physical body's mind.

Balance and offset the instincts . . .

up to the present, we have been governed by physical body instincts. The instincts are modes of behavior, which are intended or shaped to insure survival of the individual and the species.

A free spirit mind is not going to derail or erase the instincts, but the spirit mind can bring a greater degree of rationality into the process of survival. This action from the spirit mind will be welcome, because as we have seen, instincts can be "blind" and irrational. (Instincts often act in such a manner that they endanger survival) !!

Let me assure my reader at this point : a free spirit mind is not going to interfere with survival. If anything, the spirit mind will add to the physical enjoyment and fullness of life.

* * *

These four reasons illustrate how it is valuable for us to get in touch with our spirit, our real self.

And of great importance, is the fact of uncovering the truth - the truth of who and what we really are.

WHAT IS A SPIRIT ?

What is a human spirit ? For centuries, our religions and philosophies have debated this question. Thus far, all remains speculation.

Perhaps science will someday enter the question, and provide us with some hard information, as a result of repeatable demonstration.

To form our ideas about the spirit, we have only evidence from empiric and testimonial sources. I have found the testimony of Edgar Cayce to be one of the best sources for my ideas. (Edgar Cayce was one of the great American psychics).

In this book, I portray the human spirit as an entity, who is a body, a mind, and a personality. This entity has the odd ability to enter and mesh with the body of the Homo sapiens primate. This primate is also a self-aware entity.

To understand what "mesh" means, think of the way that water is absorbed by a sponge. The spirit is the water, and the Homo sapiens body is the sponge.

When the spirit meshes into the primate, a bonding occurs. This is so strong, that the spirit comes to think it *is* the primate.
The spirit thereby falls under the control of the primate's instinct programs.

Let us start at the beginning. Here are my speculations about the spirit's origin, and what has happened since.

I think the body of the human spirit is composed of a kind of matter which is invisible to the Homo sapiens' sight. That kind of matter could be similar to radio or TV energy waves. Many energies are invisible to the Homo sapiens' senses.

This concept leads to the idea that planes of energy exist, in which entities are formed. There may be many such planes.

In my proposal here, the human spirit was formed in one of these planes, and the spirit matured there.

Let us call this plane, where the human spirit was formed, and then matured - by the term "Plane of Spirit Energy".

My further thought, due to the basic nature of the human spirit, is that the spirit's nature was always one of great innocence and peace. The spirit has never been aggressive.

For this first era of the spirit's life, while it lived in the Plane of Spirit Energy, I term the spirit as "Innocentis Spiritus".

When the spirit migrated into the next era of its life, and it began to reside in the Homo sapiens body, I then call the spirit by the term, "Homo Spiritus".

* * *

The second era of life for the human spirit, began with its entry into the present plane of energy.

The spirit entered the present plane, which is termed the "Molecular Plane of Energy". We all live here, and are familiar with this plane.

In the Molecular Plane, the spirit found the Homo sapiens, and was able to enter and mesh into that primate. Thus, our spirits became, what I call the Homo Spiritus entities. And here we remain.

For those readers interested, Edgar Cayce related the details of our spirit's entry into the Homo sapiens primate.

We are still residents in the Homo sapiens primate, and still quite unaware we and the primate are two individual entities.

* * *

In the coming era of the human spirit's career, I term the spirit as the "Sapere Spiritus" - which means "wise spirit".

The spirit will be wise, because it will have learned that it is not the primate.

In the new era, Sapere Spiritus will cease to be governed by the primate's instinct programs.

This does not mean that the primate will be harmed, but that it will be the one who is governed.

The primate will become our beloved pet, and be treated with every kindness.

We will continue to reside in the Homo sapiens, but we human spirits will be the masters.

OUR BELOVED PET

As spirits, our present situation is that we reside in the body of the Homo sapiens primate, but we are unaware of so doing.

We believe, instead, we are the primate.

This mistaken identity is caused by our intense proximity and bonding to the primate body. Our mistaken identity has endured for thousands of years.

This mistake has caused us to be governed by the primate's instinct programs.

The programs have proved to be quite efficient survival mechanisms, inasmuch as Homo sapiens now dominates his earth setting. His remaining competitors are insects, bacteria and viruses, and himself.

One of the defects of the instinct programs, is violence/aggression. Homo sapiens has a long history of blood-letting.

When I see the male chimpanzees go into rage displays, or go to war on other chimp groups, I see this also in the Homo sapiens. (Too bad the Homo sapiens did not get a bit of the gorilla's peacefulness).

The only way we spirits can free ourselves from being governed by instincts, is to become aware of our true identity. We can then separate from the Homo sapiens, while remaining a resident in his body.

In effect, the process of that separation produces a kind of split-personality. The product of this is two independent minds, in one body.

A split-personality of this nature demands that the wiser half of the split, be the chief decision-maker.

The wiser half is Sapere Spiritus.

As my reader will recall, Sapere Spiritus is the name I give to spirits who have become aware of their true identity.

Sapere Spiritus, Mr. Wise Spirit, must be the one who sets the course and is the chief decision-maker.

Sapere Spiritus cannot continue to be governed by instinct programs.

Wisdom is that we, as Sapere Spiritus, will make Homo sapiens into our beloved pet. As a pet, he will be given the very best care.

As that pet, however, he will not be allowed violence, over population, greed, or other defects which have marred his life.

THE NEW AGE

Let me repeat some of what has been said.

We humans are spirits, who began life in another plane of energy, which is called the Plane of Spirit Energy.

In that plane, we had an easy life, because no work was demanded of us. Our spirit/matter bodies absorbed nutrition directly (much as the Homo sapiens bodies absorb oxygen from the air).
We spirits continue, at present, to absorb energy from the Plane of Spirit Energy ; we do not get nutrition from the Molecular Plane.

The Plane of Spirit Energy has no predators. That meant, we were not exposed to violence or aggression. We matured into peaceful entities, who were very innocent. This is why I term the early spirit as Innocentis Spiritus.

We matured in the Spirit Plane, and grew curious about the great world outside ourselves.
Our curiosity led us to migrate into the Molecular Plane, where we encountered the Homo sapiens. We found that we were able to mesh into the Homo sapiens, and have been doing that now, for thousands of years.

We paid a price, though, for our curiosity. We forgot who we really are. This was caused by the powerful force - of the Homo sapiens animal instincts.
Those instincts became our masters, and we bowed down to them.
That was our big mistake. We lost touch with our true identity.

* * *

Our lives as residents in Homo sapiens bodies, caused us to become Homo Spiritus. That term means, we have lost our innocence, and have learned violence. We took on the nature and personality of the Homo sapiens primate.

Our innocence is gone, forever.

Now, even in the periods we spend between physical body lifetimes, we are aggressive, fearful, etc.

Our thousands of years as Homo sapiens "act-a-likes", have been years of much hardship and sorrow.

At present, we remain in the Homo Spiritus mode.

* * *

Gradually, our two minds, the spirit mind and the mind of the body, are coming to realize that there is a human spirit, and it is not the physical body.

This realization paves the way for us to become Sapere Spiritus. That term means "wise spirit".

As we become Sapere Spiritus, we rediscover our true self, which will open a new world to us.

The new status will allow us to stop being controlled by the animal instincts.

We will become masters of our destiny.

As yet, only a few persons have become Sapere Spiritus. In time, more will evolve, and all cultures, and the entire earth, will enter into a "new age".

MAGIC WORDS

The human spirit can be revealed, by the technique given (please refer to pages 9 and 10). The spirit will be encouraged to express itself openly, when one uses the technique.

In time, the spirit will cease to identify itself as the physical body. As that identification ends, the spirit will approach the state of being a Sapere Spiritus.

There is a question . . . are there other means to assist the above transformation ?

Yes, there are other means. However, those means are aimed mostly at assisting the technique.

These means, in themselves, do not encourage the spirit to express itself and become independent.

We should use these means, though, because they make it easier for us to use the technique efficiently.

There are four ways to assist the technique - and are given as follows . We should "immerse" our consciousness in these four areas of activity .

(1) Maintain a peaceful mind at all times.

(2) Spend time appreciating, and/or creating things you feel are beautiful.

(3) Strive to arrive at the truth about yourself, others, and situations.

(4) See all persons, other life forms, and situations - in the warmth of compassion.

These four activities are four "magic words".

They are peace, beauty, truth, and compassion.

Employed daily, and as constantly as one can manage, the use of the words will work magic.

QUESTIONS AND ANSWERS

(1) Question :   How do you really know the human spirit exists ?

Answer :   We have no repeatable demonstrations, for or of the human spirit.   Therefore, we have no real proof.

We do have a huge mass of testimony, which indicates existence of a human spirit. In being personal, I accept the testimony, and in particular I accept the statements of the psychic Edgar Cayce.

Perhaps someday, we will invent a scientific means to photograph the spirit, or find some other way of recording it, for all to see.
Some type of recording would be indisputable.

I believe we will discover the right frequencies, or combination of frequencies, to produce such a recording.

(2) Question : Your writing of the spirit is not religious. Why not ?

Answer :   I am trying to describe, and analyze, something (the human spirit), which I believe exists.
Also, we need to solve the fact that people believe they are the physical body. In my view, the spirit and the physical body are two independent entities.

So - I think the real work is to separate the two entities, in such a way that the spirit can speak for itself.
This does not appear to be religious.   It is much more psychological.
It is a case of mistaken identity, a mistake that needs correction.

It is unnecessary to make this into a religious controversy.

(3) Question : would you please explain more about the four magic words .

Answer : The four magic words are : peace, beauty, truth, and compassion. These words are open to many personal interpretations. Let me give my meanings for them.

Peace . . . means that your mind is calm and quiet.
The mind is not agitated or excited.

There are two things which break the calmness of the mind. Those two are experience (or promise of) great pleasure or great pain.

When one of these is present, one's mind normally will not remain calm.

These two experiences are rather infrequent, so that the mind can and should remain calm most of the time.

Minds often mistake symbols or representations of pleasure and pain for the reality of those.

This mistake usually causes the mind agitation.

We are continually getting deceived by symbols.

A large part of keeping the mind calm, is to learn that symbols are representations, but not the real thing.

Beauty . . . ideas about beauty, vary widely. My conception of beauty is : beauty is harmony.

Harmony, or disharmony, enters into whatever we do, think, or sense.

Example : a low, brownish house is harmonious in a forested setting. A bright, pink house, would be inharmonious.

Another example can be found in music. Some combinations of sounds are not harmonious, and hurt one's ears. That is called dissonance.

Mozart wrote a piece which was meant to be dissonant.

Our actions, too, can lack harmony. Acts of greed are inharmonious. Whereas, generosity pleases, and creates harmony between people.

When harmony is achieved in anything, we sense beauty. And this has the additional power of uplifting our emotions toward pleasure.

<u>Truth</u> . . .   is the "what is" of anything.

Truth very often comes in layers. One layer is under another, under another, and so on. We peel off a layer of truth, only to find another layer of truth under that.

To be radical, we continue to peel away layers, as long as we can.

The value of science, is that it makes us try to reach the deepest layers.

To mention symbols again -   our culture is highly involved in the creation of symbols, which are mistaken for what they represent.

Such mistakes are untruths. Unfortunately, these untruths regularly pass for truths.

<u>Compassion</u> . . . is our sense of "one-ness" with other people, and other life-forms. This closeness enables the compassionate person to understand a need for help and sympathy, and to extend those whenever possible.

It should be understood, compassion is not bonding, because that demands a long-term very close relation between two (or a very few) individuals.

(Question # 3, continued)

When the four magic words are a strong part of one's daily life, they help create a character of mind which is receptive to contemplation of spiritual ideas.

Once a person has discovered his or her spirit self, the four magic words continue to have their beneficial effects.

(4) Question : my mind likes to dart about, so that I am a person who notices everything. How can I calm my mind ?

Answer :   You have an alert mind -   that is good.
    An alert mind is not necessarily agitated. You can be calm and yet be alert.
    Mental agitation arises when we get exicited about pain or pleasure. But even those experiences can be seen calmly, if one sees them in the perspective that excitement is a passing event.

The "long view" of time tends to calm a mind. And on the other hand, people who have a "short view", feel pressured by time, and are consequently agitated a great deal.

(5) Question :   I am a woman ; why is the sexual relation so important to me ?

Answer :   The sexual relation is much more important to women than to men. This is the case, because large elements of the physical female body, mind, and life-goals -   are devoted to child-bearing and rearing.

(Question # 5 continued)

Sexual relations are an integral part of child-bearing and rearing, and therefore extremely important to you.

This degree of importance is completely natural and normal for the female physical body.

(6) Question : does sexuality hinder me from discovering my spirit self ?

Answer :   Discovering one's spirit self (one's true self), is all a problem of making the time to work for that discovery.

If your time is used up for other activities, you leave no time to find yourself.

We are usually very inclined to use up our time on whatever gives us pleasure (or power). So - sexual activity, or many other activities, can prove so attractive that we fail to provide the time for self-discovery.

It is your choice, to decide what is important to you, to decide how to spend your time.

I should add, that any activity which strengthens one's belief that he or she is the physical body -   will naturally act to slow one's work of self-discovery.

You cannot serve two masters. You either move toward maintaining your present belief you are the physical body ;   or, you work to find out that you are not that body.

(7) Question : I am doing a lot of sports. How will this affect my spirituality ?

Answer : Let me define spirituality. It is a working self-identity as a spirit being.

A general rule is, to become spiritual : the more energy invested into physical body activity and identity, the more one will remain identified as the physical body.

Sports pulls you toward intense physical body identity. That seems to be well-nigh inevitable.

Perhaps you should re-evaluate the importance you are giving to your sports.

(8) Question : What is meant by making the physical body a beloved pet ?

Answer : Though you can become a Sapere Spiritus, you will still live in a physical body.

That body becomes your responsibility, to care for it and maintain it properly.

The new relation with the physical body, makes it a beloved pet.

Always, you give your pet dog or cat the best of care - your physical body demands even greater loving attention.

You will find, that the physical body has a strong will. And you, as a Sapere Spiritus, will need to control this highly independent animal.

This control will not always be simple or easy.

(9) Question :   I have accumulated credit card debt. Will this interfere with my attempts to become spiritual ?

Answer :   Your debt indicates that you have not mastered your economic circumstances.
   Pay off the debt, which will take time. Then, get your income and outgo in balance, so that you stay out of debt.
   After that is done, you are free to begin your spiritual study.

   In other words, when you start a drawing, begin with a clean sheet of paper.

   The study and use of the four magic words should be applied as soon as possible.

(10) Question :   I'm getting no response from my spirit self, when I talk to it.

Answer :   We all must expect this study to require time and patience.
   The spirit thinks it is the physical body. This causes the spirit to think you are talking to someone else.
   The same thing happens in normal life, when you speak to someone, and they think you are talking to someone else. The person you address, won't answer.

   Your talking to your spirit (in effect, to your real self), will be made stronger when you also spend time thinking about this odd situation. The odd situation is our spirit's taking the identity of the physical body.
   Continued thought about this oddity, causes your unconscious mind to store up a fund of information about the spirit. This fund acts as a kind of pressure on the spirit, to make it stop identifying as the physical body.

(11) Question : do you have any prediction about the future ?

<u>Answer</u> ; No - I am not a prophet. And, the future is not something determined.

But, there are two major elements that now exist world-wide, and these elements will have their effect on our future.
The two are : (1) preparations for war continue ; (2) there is an increase of trade, communications, and investments between nations, all of which is creating a "one world" situation.

It is a question of whether we will reach a strong enough one world, so that no one wants war - or whether a great war will break out before we can attain a strong one world condition.

Common sense dictates that humanity should not allow the use of nuclear weapons, which now await in their silos.
But, does humanity have a good record for using common sense ?

(12) Question : how much change for good can be made by persons who become Sapere Spiritus ?

<u>Answer</u> : That amount of change depends upon how many persons become Sapere Spiritus.

No doubt, each Sapere can do good, and if there are a few million Saperes, the earth can be saved.

BOOK TWO

Human Spirit Rediscovery

PREFACE

Almost everyone labors under a false indentification. We believe we are the physical body and its personality.

But we are not this body.
We inhabit it.

We are a spirit matter body, which has its own mind and personality.
The physical body is not animated by the spirit. Each body has its own life force. Each body animates itself.

In this book I will write about our spirits, where they come from, what they were like originally, and what they have become.
We can remedy and improve what we have become. My program to affect that improvement will be explained.

Is there purpose to rediscover who we are ?
There is good purpose. First, we should always seek the truth. And secondly, that truth will enable us to control ourselves.
During our history on earth, we have not controlled ourselves. We have been controlled by the physical body's instincts. That has not been entirely a pleasure.

Our need, and possibly our next step in evolution, is control of ourselves. Each of us needs to become master of his life.

Control of ourselves means that the spirit self is able to stand aside from the physical body self.
The two selves, the two personalities, will be aware of each other.
Decisions made will then be mutual, and not completely from the viewpoint of the physical body, as done at present.

When the two entities are aware of each other, when the spirit self and the physical self can recognize each other, we will attain a greater reality.

From this attainment, we can arrive at better decisions about our life. We will no longer be in states of compulsion, which are results of our being in thrall to physical instincts.

In our new state, we will take better care of the physical body.

In the past, it has been terribly abused.

I like to think of the physical body as a beloved pet. We give our pets the best of care possible.

Thus, my reader will see that rediscovery of our true self, and the consequences of that, are most beneficial.

Edgar Cayce was, and remains, the pre-eminent American psychic. From his thousands of trance states, he relayed much valuable information to us. It is unknown who spoke through him.

In this book I have used some of the information he gave.

Of particular interest is his story about how our spirits came to this earth, and what happened to us.

Thank you, Edgar Cayce.

Part One

THE OUTLINE

The type of outline I will use to explain my thoughts, will be a series of questions. As these are answered, it will become clear how we each can rediscover he is a spirit, not a physical body.

That rediscovery is the aim of this book.

The questions to be made are as follows :

(1) Where did we originate ?

(2) How did we come to inhabit the Homo sapiens body ?

(3) What happened to our spirits since we came to live on earth ?

(4) Why did our spirits become animalized ?

(5) How can we cease to be animalized ?

(6) What does it mean to be master of one's life ?

* * * *

Part Two of the book will be used to give a more developed explanation of the above questions 5 and 6.

TERMINOLOGY

The following terms are used in this book.

<u>True self</u> :   our real, or true, self is a spirit. It is not a physical body.

<u>Spirit body</u> :   our spirits are three dimensional bodies, composed of the matter found in the Spirit Plane.

<u>Physical body</u> :   (also called the animal body) - is the Homo sapiens body. It is composed of the matter in the Molecular Plane.

<u>Self</u> :   is the sense of being separate from the environment. As a sense, a self is dependent upon some form of body, and is a product of that body.

<u>Universal energy</u> :   is the basic "stuff" of the universe. All variation of energy is composed of universal energy. It is impersonal.

<u>Plane</u> :   is a gigantic area in which universal energy manifests in particular and unique ways. Some planes are compatible, others not.
We do not know how many planes there are.

<u>Spirit Plane</u> ;   is that energy plane wherein we spirits originated.
The Spirit Plane is compatible with the Molecular Plane and the Astral Plane.

<u>Molecular Plane</u> :   is the energy plane where we now reside in the Homo sapiens bodies.

Astral Plane : upon death of our host Homo sapiens body, we move into the Astral Plane.

Entity : is a body of some kind, which has produced a mind, a personality, and a sense of self.

Instincts : are genetic traits which are directed toward survival goals, or representations of those goals.
The animal body is controlled by its instinct programs.
The spirit body does not have instincts.

Homo Spiritus : this is a new name I coined for the human spirit. The spirit now identifies itself as the physical body and personality. As a result of that, the spirit has become "Homo", denoting that it has taken on a manlike or primate nature.
The human spirit has not changed physiologically. It has changed psychologically.

Encapsulation : records of experience can become held in the unconscious level of a mind, in a "capsule".
Those records are thereby sealed off from conscious awareness.

Mind : all minds are products of a body. No mind is self-contained.
The Homo sapiens body and the spirit body each generate a mind.
There is no universal or infinite mind.

Innocentis Spiritus : a new name coined for the human spirit, as it existed in the Spirit Plane, long ago. The name indicates that the spirit was innocent and naive.

(Terminology - continued)

Animalization : the human spirit became animalized when it took on the nature of the animal body. This happened because the spirit lost its awareness of itself, and began to think it is the animal body.

Thus, we became governed by the animal instincts.

Bonding : an entity bonds with another entity, or several, when a persistent exchange of energies takes place. Two or several entities can become almost one with each other, or feel that they are as one.

An entity can do the same thing with a locale, or with a profession.

Sapere Spiritus : my coined name meaning "wise spirit". The human spirit will one day become aware of its true self, and surmount its present animalism. When that happens, the human spirit will be wise and able to stand outside Homo sapiens, mentally, and give directives.

Sensory data : is sensation from the body senses, either from the Homo sapiens body or the spirit body.

The data contacts the unconscious, the subconscious, or the conscious mind. When the contact is made, the data will be interpreted, usually in a way of which we are unaware.

In application of the word "truth", one attempts to become aware of the interpretation, so as to separate it from the data received.

ORIGIN

In the outline given on page 1, the first question was : where did we originate ?

The answer is that we originated in the Spirit Plane.

We humans are spirit bodies, which are composed of the Spirit Plane matter.

To extend that claim, all bodies which originated in the Spirit Plane are composed of its matter.

My reader naturally wants to know more about our origin. For example, what were we like during our stay in the Spirit Plane ?

What kind of life did we have there ?

Why did we migrate into the Molecular Plane, and what keeps us here ?

Before answering those questions, I want to say that our origin was not due to the work and will of any entity -   of any God or otherwise.

In my opinion, I think our spirit bodies were formed by the interactions of the forces in the Spirit Plane. This occurred impersonally. No entity was involved.

Let us look at the questions above.

What were we like, during our stay in the Spirit Plane ?

We were naive, trusting, and childlike.

The word "innocence" describes us well.

Our innocence was due to the nature of the Spirit Plane. It contains no hostility. It has no predators.

And too, we did not have to work. We absorbed nourishment, much like the fish in our waters. They absorb their oxygen and do not have to make it.

Ours was an easy life in the Spirit Plane. Lack of danger made it unnecessary for us to develope any mechanisms of survival.

That lack of threat allowed us to remain innocent and trusting. But it did not prepare us for life in the Molecular Plane.

Our state of mind in the Spirit Plane was balmy and idyllic.

At present, our musings about a "golden age" may well arise from deep memories of our earliest life.

Why did we migrate into the Molecular Plane, and then stay here ?

I think we became adventurous and curious, as we matured in the Spirit Plane.

We wanted to look around, to poke into things, to test the unknown.

And we did. We were able to pass into the Molecular Plane, which is compatible with the Spirit Plane.

What causes us to remain in the Molecular Plane ?

The great American psychic, Edgar Cayce, sheds some light on this.

Cayce said that at first, our spirits were able to travel back and forth between the two planes. But, we became "bonded" to life in the Molecular. We became unable to return to the Spirit Plane.

We remain in that situation today.

THE HOMO SAPIENS

The second question on page 37 was : how was it that we came to inhabit the Homo sapiens body ?

An answer to that question was revealed in the statements made by Edgar Cayce from his trance. He said that once our spirits came into the Molecular Plane and became bonded with earth conditions, a group of entities called the "White Brotherhood" created a body for we spirits to inhabit. That body was the Homo sapiens, which we now inhabit.

According to Cayce, we spirits, prior to creation of Homo sapiens, were making fools of ourselves. We inhabited rocks, trees, animals, etc., and in general acted in a silly and confused manner.

Cayce mentions a "School of Beauty", where the Brotherhood performed surgery on the spirit inhabited bodies. Horns, hooves, tails, etc., were removed. Cayce does not make it clear just how and when this surgery was done.

According to Cayce, the Brotherhood took primates from five separate places and performed changes to make those primates into the present day kinds of Homo sapiens.

Today we see the result of that, in the races. Homo sapiens wears several differing kinds of bodies.

Cayce says that the creation of Homo sapiens was done to give we human spirits a suitable "vehicle" in which to live and develope.

Homo sapiens has been a good vehicle, inasmuch as he is a very intelligent animal.

HOMO SPIRITUS

The third question of the outline is . . . what happened to human spirits since we came to live on earth ?

As mentioned, we ended up as the inhabitants of Homo sapiens.

At first, we may have been able to stand aside from the animal body, and observe its actions. We probably could see, during our initial residence in Homo sapiens, that we were not him.

But as time passed, we grew to identify with and as the animal. We lost our ability to stand aside and observe.

Once we lost that ability, the animal's desires and instincts were thought to be our own. That meant, we could not question the desires and instincts. We were completely controlled by the animal's nature.

This change was a deep change in the psychology of the spirit.

The human spirit became (psychologically) a changed entity.

The human spirit became Homo Spiritus.

We took on manlike, primate qualities.

We were no longer the simple and innocent spirits who first entered the Molecular Plane. Today, we remain Homo Spiritus.

It is our present condition we must confront. We cannot return to the past. We can never again be the naive beings we once were.

Now that we are animalized (having the psychological nature of the Homo sapiens animal), its instinct programs govern our every action.

All world cultures, religions, governments, etc., are derived from our subservience to the animal's instincts.

Humanity is now saturated by the instinct programs, and no voice is heard that asks us to rediscover ourselves.

ANIMALIZATION

The fourth question in my outline is : why did our spirits become animalized ?

The answer involves a principle.
Which is : a mind is shaped by the information it receives.

Our spirit mind has been shaped for many centuries by the constant and forceful absorption of sensory data from the physical senses.

The spirit body also has senses, which channel information up into the spirit mind. However, nearly all that information is about physical conditions. In addition, our intimate contact with the Homo sapiens body and its senses, channels sensory data from the physical sense organs. Our spirit minds are bombarded with information, and almost all of it is about physical conditions.

The information we spirits receive, is about the physical world and the Homo sapiens body.
That information has shaped the spirit mind.
It is no wonder that the spirit mind thinks it is the animal body.
Our animalization was a natural result of the entry into the Homo sapiens body.

The chart on the next page illustrates the flow of physical sensory data into the spirit mind.

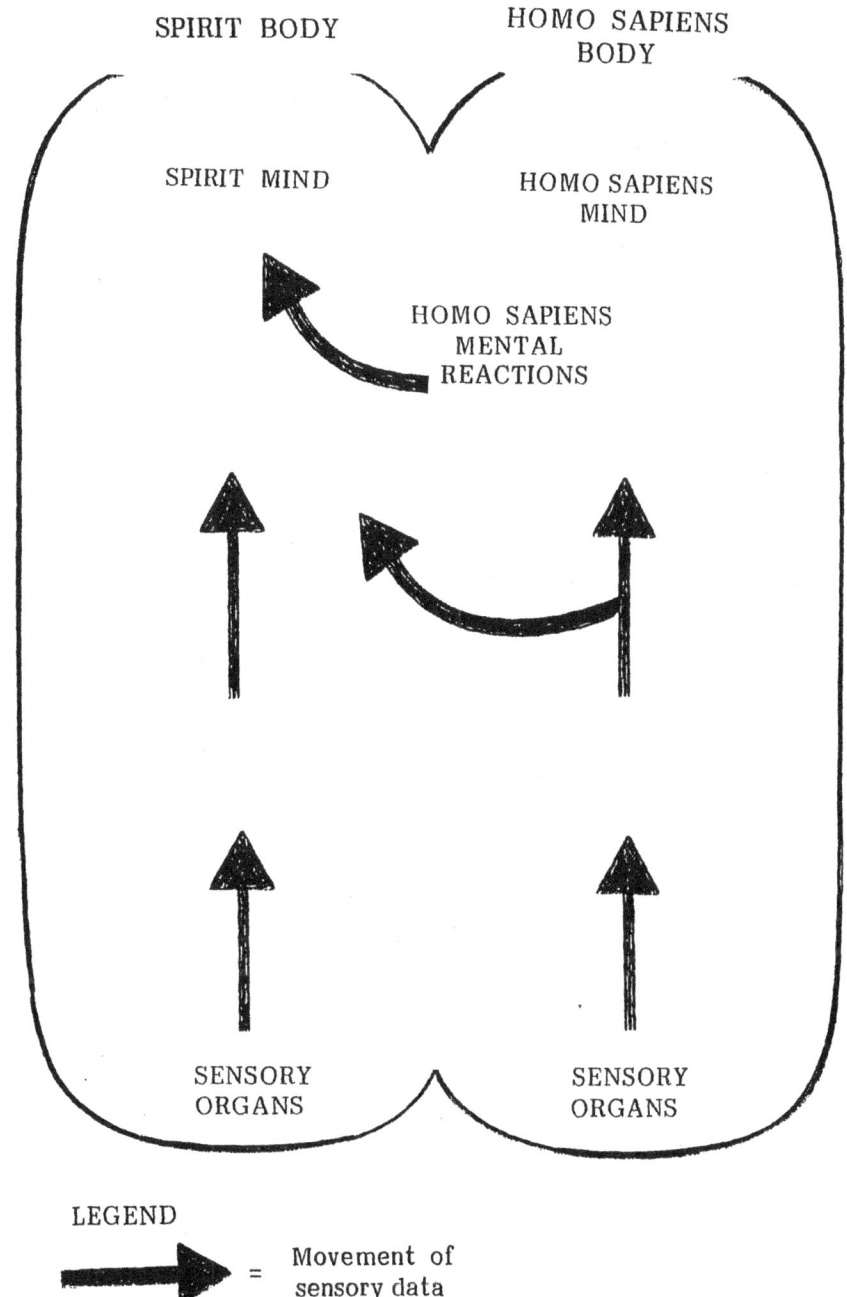

Page 50

CHART

The sensory data in the chart on page 50, comes mostly from the senses of the Homo sapiens body.

This data moves into both of our minds (both the mind of the Homo sapiens body, and also the mind of the human spirit).

Each of these two minds has an unconscious level, as well as the subconscious and the conscious levels.

The mental reactions of the Homo sapiens are carried over into the mind levels of the spirit. These reactions can come from any one or all of the three levels of the Homo sapiens' mind.

The object of the chart is to show that the spirit mind, all levels, is flooded with Homo sapiens' sensory reactions. The spirit mind will receive so much of this sensory data, this Homo sapiens data, that the spirit mind quite naturally is shaped by physical body data.

A mind is shaped by the information it receives.

The spirit mind has been shaped, in our physical world, by the physical data it receives.

The spirit mind has been saturated by physical world data, and so, the spirit mind evolved into "Homo Spiritus" : which means that the spirit mind became the present day animal-like mind.

THE CORRECTION

The fifth question of the outline is : how can we cease to be animalized ?

Thus far with these questions – we have seen that a human is a spirit, not a physical body. And the mind of the spirit has become animalized – which means that the spirit thinks it is a physical body.

Our animalization has been caused by the preponderance of physical information flowing into the spirit mind. Nearly all that information has to do with physical information, or with the Homo sapiens' reactions to physical information.

The spirit mind is saturated with physical information, and very little else. As remarked, it is no wonder we think we are the animal and its body.

To correct our dismal mistaken identity, we need to recall who and what we are. We are spirits.

First we recall. Then, that ability will enable us (mentally) to stand aside, or outside, the animal mind.

We can stand outside the animal mind, and still inhabit the animal body.

The value in standing outside the animal mind, is that we can then question, and countermand, the animal's decisions.

As we are able to question and countermand, we can issue our own decisions.

We will free ourselves from subservience to the animal's instincts.

In other words, we will end our animalization.

Let me assure my reader, no disrespect is intended toward the Homo sapiens and its mind, by my words here. The Homo sapiens is a wonderful animal, and one that is what we spirits needed for our life here on the earth.

As my reader will see, my plan and desire is to continue inhabiting the Homo sapiens - but to make radical improvements in our life.

* * * *

Part Two of this book will give a program intended to help a person recall his true self.

The program is very simple and direct. It requires no special devices, teachers, or training.

Part Two will also further elaborate on the sixth question, which is about one's becoming master of his life.

LIFE MASTERY

The sixth question of the outline is ; what does it mean to be the master of one's life ?

The answer below names the important elements of one's life. Control of these is equivalent to mastery. The most important element is given first.

(1) The most valuable element to gain in one's life is - the full awareness of one's true self as a spirit, and thereby freedom from subservience to animal instincts.

(2) Control of the health and welfare of the Homo sapiens body one occupies.

(3) The ability to benefit others.

It should be admitted that none of us will become total masters of life. We are not that powerful. Let us realize, the universe is far bigger then we, and able to provide us with surprises.
However, in our way, we can make very large improvements in our present situation.

Part Two

THE PROGRAM

The program given here, to rediscover our true self, is simple. It has but four words to be memorized.

The four words are : peace, beauty, truth, and compassion.

In the application of this program, we will use only the definitions of the four words as given below.

- Definitions -

Peace : is having a sense of eternity.

Beauty : is enjoyment of the harmony and unity evidenced in the universe.

Truth : is the ability to differentiate one's sensory input data, from one's interpretations of that data.

Compassion : is tender regard and concern for all forms of life.

Let me repeat, that one who undertakes my program should use only the above definitions.

And now, how does one apply the four words ?
First, memorize the definitions.
Secondly, study the words and ascertain how they work in your life.
Third, apply the words in your actions. You will invent personal ways for this.

* * * *

The four words represent the conditions of our early life in the Spirit Plane. That life was free from danger and demand. We then had a childlike, direct view of our existence . . . as is sometimes seen in our earth children. The word innocence describes this state.

The four words help to move our minds toward the sense of innocence. As that sense is achieved in one's mind, it resonates the encapsulated early life personality.

When the capsule is resonated, memories and sensations of our Spirit Plane life will slowly rise into consciousness. Those sensations will accrue, so that we begin to realize we are spirits, and not the Homo sapiens bodies.

Application of the four words will, in time, become a way of life. That will continue, even after one has realized his true self.

The four words in application provide a firm and sublime life-style.

* * * *

As said, the purpose of the program is to uncover our true self. And that is the fact we are spirit beings.

When one's true self is established, he is able to mentally stand outside the Homo sapiens personality.

Thus, a dual personality then exists in the Homo sapiens. One personality is the that of the Homo sapiens -   the other is that of the spirit.

Once that the spirit can stand outside Homo sapiens (mentally), the spirit will issue its own directives for action to be made.

It is no longer the creature of the animal's instincts.

This means, the spirit has now changed and become the wise spirit. It can be given a new name. It is the Sapere Spiritus. It is no longer the Homo Spiritus.

SAPERE SPIRITUS

In the last chapter, Sapere Spiritus made its appearance. That is the title I have coined for the human spirit who has surmounted animalism. Sapere Spiritus means "wise spirit".

If one will undergo the program given, and do it seriously, he will depart from his old role as Homo Spiritus. He will depart from his long subservience to animal ways.

Human spirits began life in the Spirit Plane. The time spent there is our first era. Those years, in earth time, are an unknown quantity.

As already described, in the Spirit Plane we were innocent. I have coined a name for the human spirit of the first era.

The name for us then, is <u>Innocentis Spiritus</u>.

We remained innocent during our stay in the Spirit Plane.

Innocentis Spiritus is a term that indicates the human spirit was an innocent and naive being.

Human spirits are now in their second era. This began when we inhabited the Homo sapiens. After we inhabited him, we took on his personality. We became Homo Spiritus. That meant our spirits had become manlike and animalized.

Our third era, I believe, may be on the horizon.

We will surmount our animalism, and become aware of our true self. We will begin to act from our spirit mind, and not be in thrall to animal instincts, as we now are.

As we leave animalism behind, we become Sapere Spiritus.

* * * *

Sapere Spiritus is wise. That means he is like an old judge. He has "seen it all". He has seen all the strategems and deceits of those who came before his court.

Like the old judge, the wise spirit has had lengthy experience with strategems and deceit. Sapere Spiritus knows Homo sapiens intimately. The wise spirit knows all about predilection for deceit and violence.

Thus, the wise spirit is able to mentally stand outside the animal, and govern it.

Sapere Spiritus will make Homo sapiens a beloved pet.

This beloved pet will be given the best of care - but not allowed to create disasters, as it has always done.

REINCARNATION

As mentioned earlier, more can be said about life mastery. That is the greater control over important elements of life. Those elements are : (1) realization of one's true self as a spirit ; (2) control of the health and welfare of the Homo sapiens body one occupies ; (3) and the ability to benefit others.

The first element of life mastery is realization of our true self.
Reincarnation reveals that as spirits we leave a dying Homo sapiens body, and are reborn later into an infant Homo sapiens.
The vital information in reincarnation, is that we are spirits !

Unfortunately, the usual interest in recall of past lives is directed toward the nature of the lives experienced.
Recall of past lives can be a good way to regain and rediscover that we are spirits, and not the Homo sapiens body.

* * * *

I want to say, though, that I feel reincarnation is inefficient.
The reborn spirit does not bring back with him the skills and knowledge he gained in his past life or lives.
The skills and knowledge drop into the unconscious, and for all purposes are irretrievable.

What seems far more desirable, is that one could stay in the same Homo sapiens body, as long as one desires.
Medical science is now working to lengthen life of the Homo sapiens and is making progress. Perhaps physical immortality (relatively) is somewhere in our future.

Remaining in the same Homo sapiens body, as long as one desires, is to me preferable to dying and returning to a new body.

If we could so remain, we would then be able to continue our progress in whatever skills and knowledge that interested us.

Death would not cut off that progress.

(Of course, it is mandatory that we would also be able to keep the Homo sapiens body in health and vigor).

As we know, medical science pursues relative immortality for us.

Another avenue to relative immortality is also available. That is the use of thought-forming. Thought-forms can deliver an immortality that is one of health and vigor.

This book, however, will not deal with thought-forming.

If my reader is interested in thought-forming, there are books available on that subject.

RESONANCE

The program which has been described (page 57), makes use of a phenomenon called resonance. That is, the program has four words which reactivate the memories of the spirit's early life in the Spirit Plane.

What is resonance ?

Resonance occurs when anything is vibrated, so that it sends forth energy waves. These waves reproduce the rate of vibration (at so many vibrations per second). This rate is called the frequency of the vibration.

If the energy waves contact something which will also vibrate at that frequency -   that thing will then be caused to vibrate at that frequency.

This entire process is called resonance.

In my program the four words vibrate at frequencies common or similar to the frequencies our actions and thoughts had, when we lived in the Spirit Plane.

Those actions and thoughts are now recordings (memories). They are encapsulated in our spirit's unconscious.

The purpose of using the four words is so that they will resonate the recordings in our spirit's unconscious.

When those recordings are vibrated strongly enough, we begin to recall sensations felt during our stay in the Spirit Plane.

This recall tells us we are spirits.
Thus, we begin to know who we are.
Our false identification as a physical body slowly fades away.

*   *   *   *

This chapter will now include my hypothesis about memory. We do not yet understand mental functions, and the energies involved. My ideas are therefore an hypothesis.

The hypothesis, however, clarifies the manner that we are able to resonate the unconscious of the spirit.

Memory

(1)   An entity's sense organs produce energy waves. These waves combine and result in thought and experience.

(2)   Some of an entity's sense organs record the above thought and experience.

   These recordings are called memory.

   The recordings each have vibratory frequency rate.

(3)   The above recordings become activated, begin to vibrate, when contacted by new incoming energy waves of the same or near/same rate of frequency.

(4)   This activation of memory gives us recall of our previous thoughts and experiences in the Spirit Plane.

PEACE

The program to rediscover our true self names four words. They are used to resonate our Spirit Plane memories. The first of the four words is peace. It is defined as having the sense of eternity.

What does that mean ?

Having a sense of eternity means, one is calm. He is not buffeted by time and its demands. He understands that in the eternal changes we experience, many things seem important - which are later found to be not as important as one had thought.

Most of us tend to exaggerate present problems, in which some small things often become falsely enlarged to great importance.
If we take the "long view", small things are judged for what they are . . . as being small and relatively unimportant.

Our early life in the Spirit Plane was one of great calm. Our early and encapsulated memories are of that state.
As we become calm and peaceful now, and study peace, we resonate the early memories.
The resonance uncovers our true self, and we rediscover who we are.

For a student of peace, here are a few practical suggestions.

Have small breaks from an activity which demands much time. In those breaks, do something unrelated to the larger activity.

Give yourself little holidays. Do something that pleases and interests you.

(Practical suggestions continued)

    Keep your living costs below your income. Avoid debt.

    Let others solve their own problems -   you cannot do it for them.

    Expect failures in whatever you attempt ; we learn from failures.

    Have several differing outlets for your creativity. Work at these outlets alternatively -   in a haphazard and unplanned manner.

    Treat all persons equally. Make no one more, or less, important than others.

    Keep an open mind. Our best asset is the ability to question.

BEAUTY

The second of the four words is beauty.
And as everyone repeats . . . beauty is in the eye of the beholder.

My definition of beauty is, that it is the enjoyment of the harmony and unity evidenced in the universe.
This definition allows beauty to remain in the eye of the beholder.

Each person sees or experiences beauty in his own unique way. We all possess similar senses, but there are differnces. Some see beauty one way, some another - and some do not seem to see it at all.

Is beauty a self-existent "thing", as some believe. I do not regard it as self-existent. It is a sensation of which we are capable.
We are able to sense the harmony and unity of things, and most of us enjoy that sensation.

Why does observing and enjoying beauty resonate early life records of our time in the Spirit Plane ?

That resonance occurs because in our early life we enjoyed universal harmony and unity strongly.
We were like children, and as we see in earth children, the childlike person usually has the beauty response quite naturally.
Also, it is noted that artists try to achieve harmony and unity in their paintings. They use those terms consciously.

Let us give ourselves to the beauty response.
It purifies and elevates.
It resonates early life memories, and we are then more able to rediscover our true self.

Some cultures observe beauty as a religion. For example, Navaho American Indians advocate a state they call "walking in beauty".

These Indians are probably not attempting to rediscover their true self, as I define it, but they do say that they purify themselves through this practise.

(To purify oneself means . . . to free oneself from coarseness, from guilt, and from unnecessary desires).

What are some ways we can "walk in beauty" ?

We can paint and sculpt - we can work in the garden - enjoy and participate in music - take walks - write poems and novels, and so on.

There is some kind of work in beauty, for everyone, if he wants to look for it.

TRUTH

The third word of the rediscovery program is truth. It is defined as the ability to differentiate one's sensory input data, from one's interpretations of that data.

The ability to differentiate, means that one separates his sensations, from his reactions to those sensations.

The two processes are not the same thing, and must be seen as two.

Sensation in not interpretation.

From this "fact of life", truth tells us that my truth can never be exactly the same as yours. Similar ? Yes, but never exactly the same.

Differentiating sensory data from interpretations of it is difficult.

This is the case, because we tend to attach words, values, ideas, and mental pictures to sensory data - <u>as soon as the data is received.</u>

If we do that, differentiation does not occur.

In many instances, we receive sensory data and attach it to judgements already made for previous data of like nature.

We thereby pre-judge the data, even before it is received.

If new and incoming data is pre-judged in this manner, we block the rational process.

(The rational process is : sensory data is not pre-judged, but it is examined carefully before decisions are made about the data).

* * * *

For the study of human spirit rediscovery, we should build up the art of separating incoming sensory data from interpretations of it.

This is definitely a skill. It will demand long practise, before it becomes daily action.

This skill is necessary in one's search for the true self.

It is necessary, because without it, one accumulates many false and imaginary conceptions. Perhaps needless to say, but our world is overly burdened with imaginary conceptions about the human spirit. In almost all cases, imagination acts to pre-judge actual sensory data. The result is a world now filled with and controlled by irrationality.

Let me add a caution.

If you don't develope the skill to separate incoming sensory data from interpretations of it - you will probably fall victim to imaginary ideas about the human spirit. They abound.

This caution emphasizes the value of truth in applying the rediscovery program.

* * * *

My reader may notice that the word truth is not said to be used as a resonance of early spirit memories.

Truth, in this program, is not meant for that use.

Instead, truth is meant to be the guardian of one's perceptions and decisions. We do not want to fool ourselves.

As the word itself implies - we want to find truth, not the kind of self-delusion so often found in spiritual subject matter.

COMPASSION

The rediscovery program's last word is compassion. It is defined as : having tender regard and concern for all forms of life.

The application of this word has the same intent as the words peace and beauty. The intention is to resonate the memories of the spirit's early life.

Why does compassion resonate those memories ?

The resonance occurs, because compassion is essentially an act of innocence. And, innocence resonates early life memories. The reasons have been explained.

The Homo sapiens' personality naturally has the quality of tenderness as is seen in Koko, the gorilla.
The student of the four word program should therefore have a fairly easy time to be tender and heighten that quality.

Compassion is not love. The two are different things.
Love involves bonding between two or several persons. But compassion does not require bonding. It is more impersonal. In fact, compassion usually contains no bonding at all.

As for the acts of love and bonding, those are Homo sapiens' types of processes.
The rediscovery program is not meant to stimulate love and bonding.

It may be news to many - but human spirits do not bond or fall in love, unless they are animalized.

SUMMARY

A human is a spirit, which is a body composed of the matter in the Spirit Plane. We originated in that plane, and our life there was our Golden Age - free from all fears of threat or harm. We led a life of innocence. We were childlike. There was no need for us to develope any survival mechanisms.

At that first era of our lives, we were Innocentis Spiritus - which means innocent and harmless spirits.

A great many of us migrated into our present plane, the Molecular Plane. We began the second and long era of our existence.

We became residents in Homo sapiens bodies.

Soon, we bonded so strongly with this primate, that we took on its identity. We came to think we are the Homo sapiens body and also its personality.

When we took on the identity of the Homo sapiens, we entered the second of our life-eras. We changed from being Innocentis Spiritus, to a spirit which can be called Homo Spiritus.

Homo Spiritus is a spirit who has become manlike, apelike.

The program given in this book is meant to restore our identity. We need to rediscover we are spirits, and not Homo sapiens primates.

At this time in our history, the rediscovery program can appeal to relatively few of us.

Those who can use the rediscovery program successfully will once again know themselves as spirits.

They will mentally stand outside the Homo sapiens, give directives, and make the Homo sapiens into a beloved pet.

When this takes place, such spirits will enter their third life-era, and become Sapere Spiritus. They become wise spirits.

Wise spirits take charge of their lives. This means they know fully they are spirits. It means, too, they control the health and welfare of the Homo sapiens body occupied. And lastly, Sapere Spiritus is able to be of benefit to others.

This is not a book about prediction - but I feel that the Sapere Spiritus enjoys earth life, and wants to continue here.

How many will attain the third life-era is an unknown. One hopes many will attain it.

QUESTIONS

Use of questions and answers serves to give some coverage to areas which were not discussed in previous chapters.

(1) Are there other spiritual disciplines which rediscover the human spirit ?

Answer : there are some that make that claim. I have studied some of them, but personally have not been satisfied. Another person, however, might find satisfaction where I did not.

So - I worked out the program in this book.
My aim in the program, is to offer something so simple that just about anyone can use it.

(2) Is your program religious ?

Answer : I don't think of it as being religious.

My program makes no appeals to a God, or Gods.
A person who uses the program is accountable to himself.
The program asks that you apply four words in your life. No one else can do that for you.

(3) Are you anti-religion ?

Answer : I don't oppose, or advocate, any religion.

Studies about the human spirit may appear religious in nature. But I see the subject as being scientific.

(4)   Why is questioning our best asset ?

Answer :   One who questions can improve himself. He can make discoveries more readily than the non-questioner.
   The questioner can also uncover mistakes, and try to correct them.
   He learns more easily, and can grow mentally.

   The non-questioner tends to remain at his status quo.

(5) Is the human spirit immortal ?

Answer :   We do not know. Some say the spirit (the soul) is immortal. But just how can anyone know that !

   My own view, tentatively held, is that the human spirit may possibly wear out and disintegrate some day. It is a three dimensional body, and as we see with all other bodies, of any nature, they eventually wear out and disintegrate.
   The human spirit's body, though, may last for ages. We have no way of discovering a spirit's age or life expectancy.

(6) Why interfere in the life of the Homo sapiens ?

Answer :   I suppose we spirits could move out and leave Homo sapiens to his own devices.
   But, it seems we prefer to remain here on earth, residents in the Homo sapiens.
   If we do remain here -   we should stop being subservient to the Homo sapiens' instincts. Those have only produced a long history of disasters.

(7) Why not use hypnosis to rediscover the human spirit ?

Answer :   I do not want to use hypnosis.

First, let me say that life regression under hypnosis has revealed we have lived past lives. Regression therapy has become more or less common enterprise, and many therapists make it their livelihood.

Regression therapy, thus far, does not advocate that the human spirit mentally stand outside the Homo sapiens, and give directives.

My objection to hypnosis (for my purposes), is that it can act as an impediment to the use of the word truth. Truth, as my reader knows, is one of the four words of the program.

Hypnosis acts as an impediment, because it puts commands into the subject's unconscious. The commands can bypass inspection.

This bypass means that the commands are not subjected to the separation of sensation and interpretation, which I require.

Post-hypnotic commands are reflexive. That is, one obeys them without conscious review, or knowing that one is so obeying.

For my program, any reflexive behavior is undesired.

My program calls for the unencumbered conscious, rational mind.

Hypnosis, or any other means, which results in reflexive behavior, is not useful in my program.

(8) Do you believed Jesus died for our sins ?

Answer : I do not hold that belief.

In fact, I am not concerned about the Bible and the beliefs one finds in it.

(9) Why are you against animal instinct ?

Answer : The questioner has misunderstood my meaning. I am against the human spirit's subservience to animal instincts.

That does not mean I am against the instincts.

The Homo sapiens animal has instincts, and will continue to have them.

Let me say this another way.

I am not against my dog's instincts.

But I don't want to be controlled by them.

In the same light, I don't want to be controlled by my Homo sapiens' instincts.

My program enables us to mentally stand outside the Homo sapiens and give directives to him. Such directives will at times supercede Homo sapiens' desires. Not all the time -   but whenever the human spirit deems it necessary.

During our history on earth, we have been controlled by primate instincts. Millions have been slaughtered. Do we want to continue that kind of history !

(10)   Is it true that the human spirit does not have instincts ?

Answer :   The human spirit does not have instincts. Let me explain.

Animal instincts are genetic traits evolved so as to produce the best chances for survival. That is the survival of the individual and the species.

But in the Spirit Plane, survival is not in doubt or question. Bodies formed in the Spirit Plane do not need or develop survival mechanisms.

(Question # 10 continued)

Another factor which made the human spirit's life simple was the spirit's lack of sexuality. Our state, in the Spirit Plane, was free from the conflicts that appear around sex.

(11) If a person has an addiction, can he use the four word program ?

Answer : An addiction/compulsion acts like a reflex.
That is, it causes an addict to be unable to separate sensory data from its interpretations.

As a result, truth is impaired. The student (one who uses the program) - is therefore a poor judge of his activities with the four word program.

The addicted student should clear away his addiction.
He will then be in a better position to practise the program.

As to addictions, there are many. People experience drinking and food addiction, sociality addiction, sex addiction, desire for fame addiction, body-building addiction - and so on.

I relate all addiction to the animal mind.
The spirit mind, in its state of being Homo Spiritus, thinks it is the animal, and thereby is also addicted.

(12) What does it mean to be "spiritual" ?

Answer : This is a much misused word. People add it to every sort of belief - system.
I define the word to mean : a full and working knowledge that you are a spirit, not the Homo sapiens body and its personality.

(13) Do you use meditation ?

Answer :   Yes -   but the meditation I use is "tailored" for the four word program.

    Let me define what meditation is .
    It is the act of quieting and calming mental activity.
    This is accomplished by focusing attention on a single thing.
    That thing can be varied : it can be a word or phrase, a mental picture, a physical sensation from the senses, an external object (like a table, a tree, etc.), or it can be some idea or thought already in one's mind.

    My tailored meditation is focus of attention only upon a single, incoming sensation from the Homo sapiens' senses.
    This is sensory input, from the ears, or the eyes, etc. Any sense will serve.
    Attention is focused and held upon that sensation .

    In my kind of meditation, focus is held and not allowed to fluctuate.
    Also, the mind remains fully conscious and is not suggestible.
    And, no other person is present during meditation.

    Once that focus is held upon a single input of sensory information, the meditator consciously tries to "catch" the moment when some level of one's mind attaches meaning (interpretation) to the sensory input data.
    It is found that a mind level will almost immediately attach meaning to the incoming sensation.
    If one can "catch" this moment of attachment, he can then separate the attachment and the sensation. He is "differentiating".
    That is what the truth word is intended to accomplish .

(14) What is the purpose of the truth meditation ?

Answer : The goal of the truth meditation is to separate one's sensations from the interpretation of them.

The reason for doing this, is so that one can observe how the mind can attach incorrect interpretations to sensations - without our being aware this is happening.

Reflexive mind-sets (so common in our world), are largely responsible for our attachment of incorrect interpretations to sensations.

These mind-sets are held in some level of the mind, in a fixated manner. They usually remain unquestioned. The are attached to sensations reflexively, so that one is not aware this is happening.

(15) Are there any drugs, herbs, mushrooms, or other things that help to succeed with the four word program ?

Answer : As far as I know, there are no substances, that can be taken into the body, that aid in use of the four words.

The four word practise requires one's clear mind and attention. The mind should be uninfluenced by drugs, etc.
So - I would say that those substances as named, are not a part of my program - and would prove to be a hindrance.

I suspect that people who want to use substances, to achieve something they think of as spiritual or enlightening, don't trust themselves. That is, they feel inadequate to do the work for themselves, and believe that a drug, or other, will give them the skill or power needed to find whatever it is they are seeking.

(16)   What is a mind-set ?

Answer :   A mind-set is a cohesive group of ideas and opinions, around a single subject.

The mind-set is felt by its possessor, to be a priori true and not to be questioned.

As incoming sensory data contact a mind-set, the set is activated. It then reacts reflexively. This means, the sensory data is judged and directives made, without any thought that the directives and judgements may be incorrect.

Reflexive responses do not allow separation of data and judgement/directive action.   We call that kind of response "prejudiced".

If no such separation takes place, there is no time nor opportunity for rational thought and examination of the data.

Reflexive response results in irrationality.

(17)   What makes you think Sapere Spiritus will do a better job of our living on this planet ?

Answer :   Sapere Spiritus means "wise spirit". I claim that he is wiser than Homo sapiens. And that because he is wiser, he will be able to do a better job of our living on this planet.

It is obvious that Homo sapiens' history reveals a notable lack of wisdom. He is forever destroying his most cherished things - he destroys his families, his possessions, his art and science, his recorded knowledge, and so on. He is a danger to himself and everything around him.

(Question # 17 continued)

Homo sapiens is unwise, because he is controlled by the primate instincts. They often act like mind-sets, and over-ride separation of sensory data and interpretation. Result : irrationality.

A tethered mind cannot be wise. The mind of Homo sapiens is tied to the primate instincts.

Sapere Spiritus, on the other hand, is wiser than Homo sapiens.
Sapere has been able to cut loose from the instincts, and be far more rational. (No one is completely rational).
The answer to question #17 then . . . Sapere Spiritus will do a better job of our living on this planet, because he is more rational than Homo sapiens. Sapere will not destroy all the cherished things.

Sapere Spiritus will make the Homo sapiens into a beloved pet.
The primate will not be allowed to destroy everything.

(18) Is democracy the best form of government ?

Answer : During its tenure, each form of government claims to be the best. Every form of government is a patchwork of agreements between the nation's citizens. As long as the agreements hold, the government works sufficiently well.

In my view, the best government, governs least. That would be the case, because the citizens govern themselves.
It follows, the smaller the number who govern themselves, the larger the role of government agencies.

If everyone were Sapere Spiritus, government agencies could become minimized. Don't hold your breath.

(19)   Should I find someone to teach me how to be spiritual ?

Answer :   Millions upon millions of people believe that we should find such teachers -   or have a religious belief that promises us some kind of spirituality.

In addition to religions, we have trance-mediums, gurus from India, psychiatrists and consultants, advisors on the TV and radio, and so on. All these are well paid to give us advice about our lives.

Certainly, a good spiritual teacher can show you some things he has learned. He may have a valuable role in your life.

But a person who seeks a spiritual teacher needs to be cautious.
I advise that the following thoughts be observed :

(1)   Don't "elevate" a teacher - don't feel he is more important or better than anyone else.

(2)   Test a teacher's ideas to see it they actually apply to you.

(3)   If a teacher asks for your money, or other compensation - you do not want him.

(20)   Please list the Homo sapiens instincts .

Answer :   Those instincts are . . .   (1) the Territorial Drive, which is the urge to get and hold something that will get him food and shelter. He considers a territory to be " his " and will fight to retain it.
(2) Next, is the Sex Drive, which is the urge to procreate ;   Homo sapiens will protect his offspring, even at great cost to himself.   (3) Third, is the Social Drive, which is the urge to form groups of his own kind.   Grouping increases his power to protect territory, or to acquire more territory. Grouping also makes possible large work projects.

(continued on the next page)

(Question # 20 continued)

(4) The fourth instinct is the "Following the Leader Drive ", which is the primate's urge to have and follow a leader. This may also be seen as a part of the Social Instinct. (5) Next, is the drive to have forms of communication, which led to language and other means of communication, such as writing and record keeping.

Instincts evolved as programs to aid survival of the group and the individual. The instincts are genetically encoded in the body cells, and as such are compulsive in the extreme.

(21) Will the Homo sapiens body be made immortal ?

Answer : That remains to be seen.

Medical science has lengthened life span. There is also on-going research about aging, the goal of which is to end aging.

We may become able to use thought-forms to lengthen life-span. This also proposes that Homo sapiens be kept vigorous.

As I observe us, we humans give every sign of wanting to stay on our earth, in the Homo sapiens body. We have made earth our emotional home.
In order to fulfill the above desire, we return again and again to earth - which is called reincarnation.
Our feelings seem obvious. We resort to this cumbersome reincarnation in order to remain in the earth setting.

Whatever our future, it is clear that our becoming Sapere Spiritus is the "way to go". So, let us get on with it.
As Sapere Spiritus people, our stay here on earth will then be far more sane.

(22) Please describe the shape, and other properties, of the human spirit.

Answer :   The human spirit is an ovoid shape. That is the case - if the spirit is the aura.

But, if the aura is an energy emanation from something inside the aura, then we don't know as yet the spirit's true shape.

Whatever the spirit's true shape, or form, it is three dimensional. It occupies space.

Other properties ; the spirit has senses. These discern light and form, sound, weight, and gravity, heat and cold, texture, motion, and not least of all, thought.

Please note - taste is not mentioned here. It is possible that the spirit does not have that sense.

The human spirit can record its experiences. These records serve in the spirit to form an unconscious, a sub-conscious, and a conscious. This is the same process that occurs in the Homo sapiens body.

The spirit's mind is also in receipt of sensory data that is almost entirely about our Molecular Plane (our physical world). That kind of emphasis on Molecular world experience shapes the spirit mind, and has also shaped the Homo sapiens mind.

Thus, the human spirit mind is now the Homo Spiritus, which is the term to describe a spirit who has become manlike, ape-like .

Homo Spiritus has bonded so intensely with Homo sapiens, that the spirit thinks <u>it is the Homo sapiens.</u>

The human spirit now responds to animal instinct, as though they were its own.

(Question # 22 continued)

The human spirit can move through space. It sometimes leaves its Homo sapiens body (this is called "out of body" experience).

The spirit is sexless and cannot procreate.
Perhaps this accounts for some of the emphasis on chastity, which is considered spiritual in several religions. Chastity is described as being pure and holy -   but sex as animalistic and somewhat vile.

As said, the spirit can move through space. It can also interpenetrate objects and bodies in the Molecular Plane. In this way, the spirit enters and occupies the Homo sapiens body.
This property of interpenetration is similar to water being held in a sponge. The spirit is held in the Homo sapiens body - and contacts the animal senses and thought processes.

This close contact, over the centuries, has evolved the human spirit into Homo Spiritus.

Life expectancy : we have no data about this. Some believe the human spirit is immortal and eternal. But that belief has nothing to substantiate it.

Nourishment : the spirit draws energy, which is its nourishment, directly from the Spirit Plane. Thus, the spirit does not have to eat and drink. For this reason, I have said the spirit may not have the sense of taste.
This drawing of energy from the Spirit Plane is possible, because the Molecular and Spirit Planes occupy the same space, but vibrate at differing frequencies (much as radio waves can occupy the same space).

Travel : movement into other planes is an ability of the spirit, but

(Question #22 continued)

only three planes seem involved : the Spirit Plane, The Astral Plane, and the Molecular Plane.

According to Edgar Cayce, we do not return to the Spirit Plane again but do draw nourishment from it. Our whole interest is now centered in the Molecular Plane.

The Astral Plane serves as an interim stop between our lives in the Molecular Plane.

* * * *

As a last word in this description of the human spirit, I should add that none of the above information is scientific. That is, it is not based on repeatable tests.

The information is based largely upon testimony gathered from many persons, over a long time period. Also, the trance information from the psychic Edgar Cayce plays an important part of the claims made.

Personally, I think the information given above is reliable and good, considering how little we know at present.

As time progresses, I am sure the subject of the human spirit will attract scientists, to gather scientific information about the spirit.

(23) You mention thought-forming. What is that ?

Answer : Thought-forming is the art of using projected thought, for the purpose of obtaining something one desires.

Thought-forming is an art, because the projected thought must be made so that it is non-negative, and non-contradictory.

Projection of the thought into the environment is done, and the projection affects the environment so as to bring one his desire.

(Question # 23 continued)

The theory behind thought-forming is that thought is a kind of energy which can be concentrated and projected out from oneself. This idea proposes that thought is an energy similar to radio wave energy, which is projected from a radio station. The stronger the energy projected, the farther it travels in space, and the more impact it has upon a receiver.

In thought-forming, one tries to concentrate his thought energy, and then use great force to project it into his environment.

The second part of this theory, is that the thought energy sent forth, will impact and resonate things in the environment, which return to the sender of the thought-form, that which he desires.

Sapere Spiritus is able to make successful thought-forms, much more often than Homo sapiens. This is because Sapere is more rational, and not subject of the instincts. Instincts can cancel thought-forms, inasmuch as instincts often promote compulsion and violence. Those elements are prone to create contradictions and negativity in thought-forms.

Contradiction and negativity cancel the thought-form.

(24) Please explain what planes are.

Answer : The theory involved in planes is that they are variations in universal energy. Each plane is a set of frequencies which give that plane unique properties.

Universal energy is, the basic energy from which all planes derive.
Universal energy is the fundamental vibrating energy. It occupies all space, or one can say it is all space.

Some planes are compatible, and share some of the same frequencies. This sharing is what allows human spirits to travel between a few planes.

(Question # 24 continued)

The sharing of the same frequency, in different planes, also allows human spirits to get their nourishment (energy) from the Spirit Plane, while at the time residing in the Molecular Plane.

It is logical to think human spirits cannot travel between all planes, inasmuch as we do not have the needed frequencies to do so. And also, it is theorized that some planes are incompatible. The presence of anti-matter suggests this.

We have only poor information about planes, and the above views are purely theoretical. There may be entirely differing explanations for what we observe.

About universal energy : it is impersonal.
It is not a person or a mind (contrary to some philosophies).
Its forces produce the universe as we see about us -   but this is not some kind of plan, or planned work.

A plane may have forces within itself which interact, so as to produce living entities. The Molecular Plane is a prime example. It has a huge diversity of life-forms.
We do not know how many planes are capable of creating life-forms.

(25) Does the human spirit animate the Homo sapiens body ?

Answer :   This is a popular misconception. Many believe the life-force of the Homo sapiens body is the result of there being a spirit in that body. That is a mistake.
The Homo sapiens, and the human spirit, each has its own life-force. Each body animates itself.

(26) What are some practical hints - about becoming Sapere Spiritus ?

Answer :   Practical hints may be practical for one person, but not for another. Let me try to address the average person.

I would say the average person, today, has too many demands upon his time and energy. So - the thing he needs to do, is to reduce the number of those demands.

One simple way to do this, is to cut some connections.

For example, you can stop use of your cell phone. It allows others to connect to you and use your attention and energy, at all times of the day. That connection should be severed.

The average person does not actually need the cell phone.

It may be a convenience, but it also increases one's connections to the world.

Cut one connection, and demand upon you is reduced.

Another kind of connection is the credit card.

You can stop using it, with no harm done.

The credit card is a subliminal message that says, "Get out and buy something !"

You do that, and you are connected again - to the whole commercial noise.

And worse, it is a trap for the unwary. Consumer credit card debt has become astronomical.

Those two examples serve to illustrate my point. Cut connections. Reduce demands upon you.

The reason one should reduce demands, is because the potential Sapere Spiritus needs first, to become a contemplative person.

He needs to make some withdrawal from the world. He does not become a hermit - but makes some withdrawal.

(Question # 26 continued)

A practical approach to becoming Sapere Spiritus, is first to assess your connections to the world. For the average person, those are increasing at a rapid pace.

Many connections are unnecessary.

Cut yourself off from them -   do some personal pruning of your mental life.

* * * *

Another element in becoming contemplative, is "refusal of emotional episodes ".

Do not enter into situations which stir up emotions.

Our prime supplier of emotional episodes is television.
Almost the entire programming of TV, accents heavy emotion.

A potential Sapere Spiritus should realize the basic nature of TV, and watch only newscasts and the occasional educational program.

There are many other sources of emotional episodes. Refuse them. Do not enter into them.
Refusal must be done, because those episodes are almost totally animalistic.
If you want to remain the creature of animal instinct - continue to engage in emotional episodes.

What you practise -   you are.

(Question # 26 continued)

Practical approach to becoming Sapere Spiritus is not difficult. One can begin with the above hints, which are few in number. The most complex hint is the refusal of emotional episodes. And that is because everyone around you will want you to join them in their little dramas.

The potential Sapere Spiritus will have to invent his own methods to refuse emotional episodes -   when confronted by those who expect his participation.

To repeat, the potential Sapere will make some withdrawal from the world. This promotes his contemplative attitude, calms the busy mind, and enhances his entry into my tailored meditation.

At the same time, world withdrawal clarifies one's use of the four word program. The program becomes better established.

BOOK THREE

Self and Basic Energy

PREFACE

This book is about our true Self, and how it is a product of the basic energy of the universe.

Basic energy is an unknown. And, probably will remain an unknown, because it may be infinite. We are unable to sense something that is an infinite. Our understanding of it is very small.

My naming the basic "stuff" of the universe, by the term of basic energy, seems appropriate.

I call it basic energy, because the universe seems so perpetually active and always on the move.

It also seems appropriate to think of the universe as a one-ness. It is entirely composed of this single stuff -   basic energy.

Were the universe made of many disconnected forces - it is logical to suppose that the universe would not have a perfect union and cohesion.

But it apparently does have a perfect union in itself.

My view of the universe is but one of many viewpoints.

And though I like my view -   intellectual honesty tells me that other opinions have equal chances of being valid.

No opinion rests upon genuine evidence, therefore all opinions are only thoughts -   based on little or no evidence.

There is ample room in this vast and perhaps infinite universe, for differing opinions.

INFINITY

What is basic energy ?
It is an energy from which everything is made.

I call it an energy . . . but no one knows what it really is.
Perhaps we can never know.

My additional proposal is that basic energy is infinite.
It has no boundaries, and it has no beginning nor ending.

Let me repeat, of course, that we cannot prove these ideas.

PLANES

Does the universe exhibit some kind of order ?

I think we can see such an order.

That order, I believe, is the system of planes which has been formed by the basic energy.

Each such plane is made entirely of basic energy.

And, the basic energy of each plane has made itself into various rates of vibration (called frequencies).

Thus, Plane A's basic energy vibrates at a series of frequencies, such as 7 - 10 - 13 - 81 - 117 .

Plane B vibrates at frequencies 4 - 32 - 98 - 44 - 79 .

And so on, with innumerable planes each having its own set of vibration frequencies.

Each plane has its own kind of individuality.

(Note : the numbers given are not meant to be the true frequencies, but are illustrations only, of each plane's uniqueness).

The plane we humans occupy at present, has been named the Molecular Plane. Supposedly, this name was used, because our plane is one which has many molecules.

In addition, we seem to occasionally inhabit the "spirit matter" plane, and also the "astral" plane.

These three planes are compatible, and allow us to enter them.

INDIVIDUATION

The Webster dictionary says that individuation is development of the individual from, out of, the universal.

We have two things to consider : there is the universal, which I call the basic energy. And we have the untold billions of varieties and examples of individuals.

My contention is, that all these individuals developed out of basic energy. They are all composed of the same energy.

It strongly appears, that basic energy has within itself, forever, a kind of pattern or pressure - which continually exerts itself to produce individuals.

This pressure exists in all parts of basic energy.

VARIETY

Basic energy is physical. The idea that it is partially non-physical is a mistaken idea. (My personal opinion).

The energy, being physical, produces everything in some kind of physical form. (Even wave-energy is physical).

The variety of what basic energy developes - is beyond anyone's comprehension.

Everything is basic energy, a physical thing, from the largest plane, to the smallest particle.

Each of the innumerable planes, contains its own set of frequencies, which interact. Thus, each plane produces its own kinds of life-forms, its materials, and so forth.

As for our plane, called the molecular plane, it produces wave-form energies, particles, molecules, and of course, our Homo sapiens bodies.

Variety of individuation, seems endless.

THE REAL SELF

Basic energy's forces create planes of itself, and each such plane has its individual set of frequencies.

These frequencies, in each plane, interact and produce the materials and qualities characteristic of that plane.

Our molecular plane has produced life-forms, of which Homo sapiens is an example.

Our bodies, in turn, are able to sense and respond to the environment, and this response causes us to form memories and values.

I call our memories and values the "peculiarities" we accrue.

The peculiarities, taken as a whole, are commonly called personality.

As we see everyday, personality is not a stable entity.

It changes radically, from childhood to age.

Personality is so ephemeral and changeable -   is it a real Self ?

Is there such a thing as a real Self ?

The changeable nature of personality tells us, it is not a real Self.

A real Self has to possess stability and remain the same, throughout a lifetime.

Therefore, because personality does not remain the same throughout a life, it is not a real Self.

Then, what is the real Self ?

Are we a real Self ?

The answer is "yes". We are a real Self.

And our real Self is that part of each individual which is the element of "pressure" (already mentioned), which exists in basic energy.

That pressure is a constant force in basic energy, which causes the production of individuals of every kind.

That formation of individuals is accomplished by interaction of the diverse forces in each plane.

This pressure, as said, is constant and in each individual.

The elemental nature of this pressure does not change or fluctuate.

We humans recognize this pressure in each of us - as present and unchangeable through all the years of life.

We refer to it as our "Self".

The smallest child will make this reference.

The Homo sapiens is an individual, and each individual Homo sapiens is a Self.

Likewise, the human spirit body, which often resides within a Homo sapiens, is also an individual and a real Self.

(It should be stated, that these two individual Selves, are not the same kind of being, but are quite different from each other).

PERSONALITY

What is a personality ?

It is an amalgam of one's memories and values.
(It has been called one's "self-image").

With most people, the amalgam does become their idea of who and what they are. The amalgam becomes a self-image.

Moreover, the amalgam is usually mistaken to be one's real Self.
But it is not a real Self.

<u>One's real Self is that pressure, that force in oneself,</u> which comes out of the basic energy.
This pressure, this force, is real. It is the cause behind our sense of being an "I am". The smallest child knows it is an "I am".

This pressure in basic energy is a pattern/pressure, to individuate itself. Thus, the universe is subject to continual individuation, in billions of varieties.

* * * *

There is an extremely common pathology, in which personality is made to respond negatively.
The negative response will be to some kind of threat, which challenges the worth and/or value of the memories and values that compose the self-image.
Negative responses to challenges vary from violence, to mental and social actions.

Yes, we humans, who believe our personalities are the real Self, are very prone to negative responses. It is our history, by and large.

We should attach a small flag to the personality, which would read as follows : "Don't tread on me".

* * * *

A student of golden light, who wants to become saintly, must learn that he is not the personality, the self-image.

That image is a construct, a false "I" - which Buddha went so far as to call an illusion.

Each of us is a real "I" - which is the pattern/pressure within the basic energy.

A WORLD PATHOLOGY

A human is very complex, in ways that often cause great pain and suffering. One such way is our insistence that personality is a true and real Self.

But, the personality is not a true and real Self.

The belief and practise that personality is a real Self, causes vast amounts of pain and suffering.

This mistaken belief is a world pathology.

So, what is the personality -   and how is it the cause of a world pathology ?

First, any personality is an amalgam of parts. The parts are two: one part is memory, and the other part is one's set of values.

These two parts combine and create the appearance of being a person, a Self.

But the amalgam is only an appearance. It is an illusion of a Self.

A genuine Self is not present in a personality.

* * * *

This belief about personality causes a world-wide pathology.
How does this happen ?

Pathology happens, because the belief creates unending conflict among all the peoples on earth.

Such conflict is caused, due to the fact that personality is derivative, and depends for its feeling of validity, upon memory and values being accepted and unchallenged.

<u>If personality (memory and values) are challenged, personality resists.</u>

And resistance varies from violence to lesser forms of action.

As said, when personality is challenged, it almost always responds with some form of resistance.

And - resistance equates as conflict, which we see world wide.

Let me make a small example.

A person, John, thinks he is very clever and intelligent.

But Mary says to John, "You are a dumb, stupid person."

The normal kind of John is immediately humiliated and hurt.

The smarter he thinks he is, the more he is hurt.

So, John finds some way to respond, usually an angry way.

He tells Mary she is not so smart herself, and in addition, she is a worthless tart.

Well - !!   The fur flies.

This conflict can be small and between two people - and it can get completely out of control, and become war between nations.

Great pain and suffering.

*   *   *   *

The personality creates a false Self, and illusion of Self.

Is there a genuine Self, which underlies consciousness, in each person ?

Yes, there is a true Self, which is each of us.

Our true Self is an harmonic of basic energy.

It is an harmonic of the pressure in basic energy to individuate.

Harmonics are, probably, infinite in scope. Thus, each of us can have a slightly differing harmonic. We see this is the case, - as no person is identical to anyone else.

Even so-called identical twins, are not really identical.

The harmonic of basic energy, which is an harmonic of the pressure to individuate, is real energy.

It is not an illusion.

Most importantly, the harmonic is no derivative from memory and values. It is totally independent of those.

Thus, the true Self does not need validation, acceptance, or agreement in order to sense itself as real.

The true Self <u>is</u> -   and knows it is.

Very few of us have discovered our true Self.

Instead, nearly everyone equates his Self with the personality, in which he is presently immersed.

Result -   we are forever engaged in some form of conflict.

SELF . . . TRUE AND FALSE

Basic energy has formed us all.

It has this great inner pressure to make individuals in billions of kinds, without end.

And here we are, humans on this earth.

Each of us a real Self, which is an harmonic of the pressure in the basic energy to individuate.

However, instead of becoming aware of our true Self, we have all come to believe we are our personality. We have come to invest ourselves in our memories and values, and think they are a true Self.

Personality enables us to make our way in the world - but is not a true Self.

It is as Buddha taught ; personality is an illusion of a Self.

My question is : why is it that we do not become aware of our true Self ?

I think this failure of ours, is due to the natures of the true Self and the personality as they are compared.

That is : the true Self is self-contained and does not advertise and promote itself. It is quiet.

Whereas : the personality is noisy and constantly advertising itself and seeking to verify that it is a Self.

True Self and personality are like two differing kinds of persons.

I think of personality as being always unsure that it is a Self.

Therefore, it is always trying to prove that it is a Self.

The personality is unlike the true Self, because the personality is forever trying to prove, it *is* a Self.

Whereas, the true Self doesn't have to prove this, and therefore does not make efforts to prove itself.

We can see this action in the personality, in so many of us.

There are millions of us who try to "find themselves". They try on one personality after another, but their state of uncertainty remains.

These unfortunates never find a true Self in personality, because there isn't one there to find.

* * * *

The true Self does not push itself forward, to prove that it exists.

It doesn't need to push.

It already knows it is a Self.

So - it is quiet, and harder to discover.

The personality is the noisy one.

Of course, some personalities make a retreat from life, and seek some kind of anonymity.

But by and large, most personalities continually seek verification.

THEORIES

The goal of my thoughts and writings, is to attain as much mental and physical freedom as possible.

That entails having an intense respect for truth.

I define truth as : receiving and being aware accurately of sensations, and making accurate comparisons of those, with sensations received in the past.

Humanity has found, thus far in history, that the scientific method is the best method yet, for finding truth.

This method first makes an hypothesis, about a solution to a problem.

Tests are made to validate, or invalidate, the hypothesis.

When a hypothesis seems to be valid, it is elevated to the status of a theory.

The theory is then used in regard to the problem originally faced.

If the theory proves insufficient, work will begin anew to solve the problem.

All this effort indicates, we should not be "sold" on some idea or a particular theory.

Many trusted theories have been found to be incorrect, and have been discarded.

Freedom requires, we keep our minds open and flexible.

HARMONICS

What are harmonics ?

They are overtone frequencies which are produced by a fundamental.

We notice these in music, where a tone is made up of many frequencies. When only one part of the tone is heard, when only one of the many frequencies is heard, we are hearing an overtone.

The overtone is also called an harmonic.

Basic energy, which composes the universe, has endless fundamentals, which produce overtones (harmonics).

One basic energy fundamental, is its inner pressure/pattern to form individuals.

An harmonic of this pressure, creates the individual "I am" in us.

Thus, our "I am" is a real energy. It is a real part of basic energy.

Our personal "I am" exists, and is a reality.

* * * *

The entire process of creating the "I am" is undoubtedly too complex for us to fathom.

We can only touch the edge of this mystery -   as we do in this writing.

GOLDEN LIGHT

Agencies superior to humanity have made programs to raise human consciousness. The programs have been somewhat successful, but of course, not totally.

We have outgrown tribalism, as it existed long ago.
Now, we have nations . . . and a world-nation is possible in our near future.
Hopefully, a world-nation will lessen warfare, and, can perhaps assure a more equal access to earth resources.

We are also in the phase of changing the punishments given crime.
Once we stoned to death for adultery - cut off the hand or hands of a thief - and so on. Very severe punishments were made.

The influence of Jesus of Nazareth has caused us to become more humane.
In many places, capital punishment is no longer allowed.

And a new concern has appeared. It is called environmentalism.
In this concern, quite a few people are trying to preserve the land, the forests, and wild-life.
Depredation of these continues, but at last is recognized as plunder.

I credit most of our consciousness advancement to the silent and withdrawn agencies, who work for the good of humanity.

And, I think, our most recent addition to programs for human consciousness advancement - is the program about "golden light".

The golden light program asks people to become saintly.

To become saintly, one must love peace, love beauty, love truth, and be compassionate toward everything.

This is a simple program.

But strenuous.

This program re-makes the mind, the goals, and the actions of those who use the program.

An important effect of being in resonance with golden light, is that it offers very superior protection, to its adherents.

Accidents are thwarted ; evil plans and designs are shunted away ; the minds of those who would do you harm, are exposed - and so on.

In addition, golden light adherents can expect support, in myriad ways, for their good.

The golden light program has just begun. A handful of people are now aware of the program.

Golden light will become widely known and practised.

As this happens, the long awaited "new age" will arrive.

QUESTIONS AND ANSWERS

(1) QUESTION

Why did Buddha teach that the Self is an illusion ?

ANSWER   Nearly everyone has always mistaken their personality for a real Self. This was as true in Buddha's time as it is today.

Buddha saw the fallacy of this and called the personality an illusion of the Self.

But he went further and claimed there was no real Self.

Possibly, Buddha was teaching the Hindu belief that there is no Self except the universe, which is sentient and the only real Self.

The hypothesis of this book is that a real Self, is in sentient entities, but not in the personality. We would say here, that Buddha was at least half correct.

(2) QUESTION

Are Buddhism and Taoism the same ?

ANSWER   No -   they are not the same.

Taoism does not have the "Four Noble Truths" of Buddhism, nor does Taoism have the "Eightfold Path".

Buddhism also has a path to enlightenment, which means, someone can become "all knowing".

Taoism does not have such a path.

(3)   QUESTION

   Does the golden light program lead to enlightenment ?

ANSWER   Enlightenment means that a person has become all knowing.

   He becomes, in a sense, infinite.
   I do not consider this to be possible for <u>any</u> entity.

   The golden light program, therefore, does not have enlightenment as a goal. But, golden light does have love of truth as a goal. That love and practise of it, clarifies the mind, making it a better tool.

(4)   QUESTION

   What about sexuality and chastity ?

ANSWER   My personal opinion is, that chastity aids one to gain control over the physical body's sex instinct.
   You master the instinct -   rather than being mastered by it.

   If you are not the master, you are usually the slave.

   Regarding children, sex is necessary and admissible, but only for the creation of children. Sex is not permissible for pleasure only.

   Chastity is almost unknown these days, in the year 2002 A.D.
   There is a rage for sex and all the symbols used to excite sex.

   I feel that the demonic forces (the dark forces), have increased the use of sexuality.

(5) QUESTION

What is wrong with obeying one's instincts ?

ANSWER

Nothing is "wrong" with obeying - and we are forced to obey some drives in order to keep the physical body alive and healthy.

The admonition to control instincts, in the golden light program, is about controlling what we can, and how much we can.
We can control the sex instinct, and control it quite a lot.
And to a lesser degree, we can control the social and territorial instincts.

The social instinct is : forming a group, being part of a group, and having or being a leader of a group.
We can control this instinct, by not following or being a leader.
As for being in a group, society in general is a group of one sort or another, and we are grouped, whether we like it or not.
But, we can eliminate much of the groupyism that is popular.

The territorial instinct is : holding some kind of property or position which generates food, care, and shelter.
Territory is a necessity for life itself.
But territory is often too enlarged, due to status seeking and/or fear problems.

Keep to a simple life, and the territory needed will not be enlarged.
The consequences of unnecessary enlargement of territory are stress, and very often the entrance into conflicts.

Be the master . . . not the slave.

(6) QUESTION

How are individuals formed ?

ANSWER   Before I state my hypothesis about formation of individuals, let me say we are dealing here with a "mystery wrapped in an enigma", as goes the old saying.

My hypothesis cannot be tested, as yet anyway, and must remain only a group of thoughts.

The hypothesis :   basic energy contains a pressure to individuate. It does so, all the time. We see countless kinds of individuals.

This said pressure is in every part of every plane.
In all planes, the many forces interact, and in so doing, are guided by the said pressure toward individuation.
That is, forces are guided to work together, in order to produce all manner of individuation.

Let me add, although all individuals are just that, and thereby become distinct from their surroundings, not all individuals are so shaped that they become aware of what they are.
We humans, and some others on our planet, are so shaped that we can be aware of being an "I am".
We are each a Self.

It is important for people to discover that they are a real Self, which is not their personal memories and values.
A deep discovery of this nature will give a person greater stability and free him from need to prove and verify that he is a real person.

(7)   QUESTION

Why aren't there special exercises and meditations for students of the golden light program ?

ANSWER   It is true -   there are no special exercises or meditations for students of the program.

There is only the simple requirement that a student understand the ideas, and try to put them into practise.

The ideas are simple.
They are : be harmless , love peace, beauty, and truth - and have compassion for everything.

In order to practise the golden light program, only your normal, daily level of awake consciousness is used.
The program may prove difficult for some, but no special exercises or talent is needed.

As for meditation, I recommend that students <u>do not meditate.</u>
(In our day and times, my recommendation seems odd, and against prevailing practises).

I oppose meditation, because its techniques are basically hypnotic.

Deep meditation can actually become a stage of hypnotic trance.

The golden light program calls for an alert and fully rational level of mind.
We do not want ourselves to enter any mental level, that makes us suggestible.

(8) QUESTION

Will golden light make me psychic ?

ANSWER   That depends upon how saintly you become .
In a very saintly person, psychism is to be expected as normal.

Let us understand . . . being psychic only means, that information flows freely from the lower mind levels, upward, and into the everyday conscious level.

In the average person, this upward flow is blocked. Blockage can be due to stress, tension, a belief system in place, and/or effects from early training in one's life.

Blockage is reduced or removed by resonance with golden light.

Blockage is reduced or removed, when the channels between the mind levels are cleared and returned to function.
(It is worth mentioning, that these channels are open in children, and not yet blocked. Consequently, small children show much natural psychism, often to the surprise of adults).

Everyone can experience constant psychism, if his channels are freed.
We should not think of psychism as miraculous or reserved for a few.

While on this subject, let me add that people who <u>are not resonating</u> with golden light, and who are psychic, may experience connections with devious and dark forces (demonic entities).
Such connection can be dangerous, if one is not aware of it.
The dark forces mean us no good   -   and will create conflict and pain if they can.

(9) QUESTION

Is the human spirit a separate being from the physical body ?

ANSWER   Yes - it is a separate being.

And, both the human spirit and the Homo sapiens physical body are individual Selves. Each is an "I am".

Thus, if the human spirit comes to reside in a Homo sapiens body, there are then two Selves, living together.

This is a "symbiosis".

Most of us are unaware of being in state of symbiosis.

That is because the spirit has identified itself with and as the physical body. The spirit <u>thinks it is</u> the physical body !

The spirit also identifies itself with and as the body's personality.

I feel we should learn to be aware of being a human spirit.

The spirit is a body composed of spirit plane matter ; and the spirit has a mind, senses, and its own personality.

Unfortunately, the spirit's identification with and as the physical body, perverts and masks the spirit's true character.

The more we learn we are spirits, then, the more the spirit mind and its character can begin to control our lives.

Such control is desirable, because the spirit lacks instincts, and has a potential of being much wiser than the physical body mind.

The lack of instincts enables the spirit to be more rational, and to avoid reflexive responses to life needs and problems.

(Reflexive responses are not desirable, inasmuch as they are thoughtless and contain latent violence).

(10)   QUESTION

What is a reflexive response.

ANSWER

A reflexive response is one of the two kinds of response we make to our daily decisions.

Those decisions, both large and small, are demanded of us throughout the day.

The reflexive response is marked by lack of thoughtfulness.

That is, it is an automatic response.

Much of what we do, daily, can be usefully and properly handled by automatic actions. We cannot possibly dwell at length over the vast majority of small actions and decisions we have to attend.

So - the reflexive response will always hold a firm place in our armory of ways to respond.

The second kind of response is the use of reasoning and comparative thinking.

In this, we delay decisions, in order to arrive at what we deem to be the best answers to our problems.

We can call this the reasoning response.

Our problem, as human beings on this planet, is that we use reflexive responses to solve problems, but they are often problems that demand the reasoning response.

An enormous amount of reflexive behavior is common in the world.

The mores of every nation are almost entirely reflexive in character, and become the guides for making serious decisions.

This is unfortunate. The result is no end of troubles.

(11)   QUESTION

   Is an instinct a reflexive response ?

ANSWER   No - instinct is itself not a reflexive response.

That is the case, because instinct is generic, not specific, whereas the reflexive response is a specific response which is determined by the nature of the personality.

For instance, the sex instinct is the urge procreate, but does not aim one at a specific sex partner. The instinct aims one at generic partners.

The personality, as it reacts to the instinct, determines what sort of sex partner is chosen.

The personality can be very unwise, and choose bad sex partners.

The existence in the world today, of 40 million people who have the AIDS virus, shows us how often we choose bad sex partners.

The golden light program advises chastity, as the answer to better control of the sex instinct.

Chastity does seem extreme to most people, but it proves to be, at least, a simple and clear method of control.

And via this control, one learns what his mind is doing, and how the mind can perform tricky and mischievous mistakes.

(12)   QUESTION

   Why try to control our instincts ?

ANSWER   If we control our instincts, we are being thoughtful, and are using reasoning responses (rather than reflexive responses).

This enables us to better approach evaluation of truth.

Learn how to love the truth.

CONCLUSION

This writing has been about the true Self, and basic energy, and how the Self is produced by basic energy.

It has been thought necessary to speak about Buddha's teaching, because he saw our normal view, of a personal Self, as illusion.

He was partially correct.

This writing is also part of a continuing discourse about golden light.

It is my hope that many of us will come to understand golden light, and enjoy its benefits.

Which would mean, such people will become saintly, and thereby help to improve the world.

In this year 2002 A.D., another war looms in the near future.

The U.S.A. flexes its powerful military muscles, while the people of Islam smoulder in their hatred of western ways.

Essentially, another endless religious war may be brewing.

It would be good for all, if golden light became a widespread practise and knowledge.

Wars, and other mistakes, could then be eliminated.

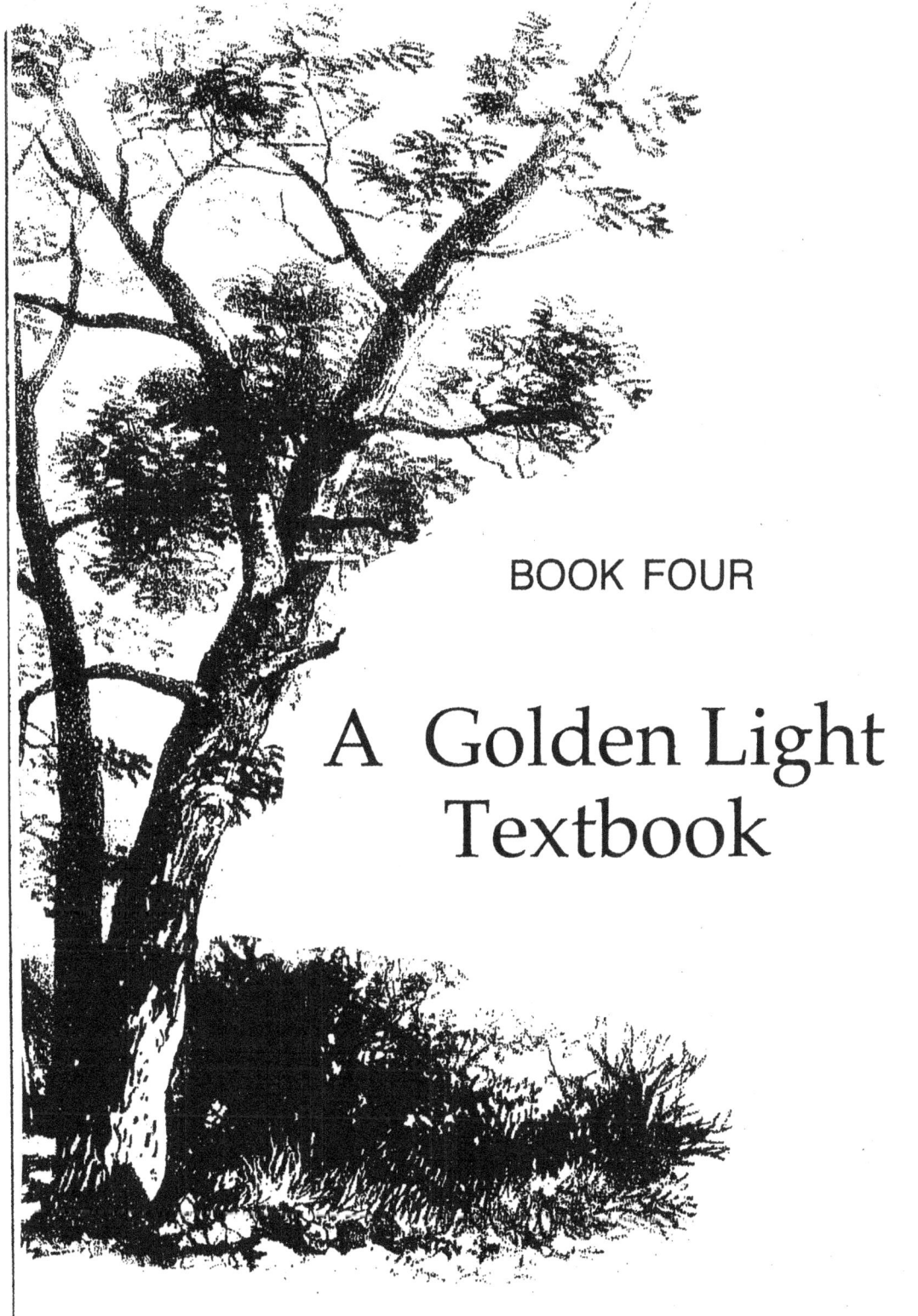

BOOK FOUR

A Golden Light Textbook

PART ONE

What is Golden Light?

DEFINITIONS

(1) **ALLY (page 141)** . . . the Ally is the great golden light thought-form, which supports and protects those who resonate with golden light.

(2) **AURA (page 149)** . . . the aura is the body of the human spirit. It is observable as being various colored light.

(3) **BEAUTY (page 181)** . . . is balance and harmony.

(4) **COMPASSION (page 189)** . . . is sympathy, mercy, tenderness, and a sharing of what others have to endure.

(5) **ENERGY, BASIC (page 193)** . . . is the "stuff" of which the universe is composed.

(6) **GOLDEN LIGHT (page 133)** . . . is the actual light emitted from the spirit bodies of higher type persons (such as Golden persons).

(7) **GOLDEN PERSON 133** . . is a person who is governed by his spirit mind. He has separated his physical body mind from his spirit mind.

(8) **INNER DIALOGUE (pages 157-158)** that dialogue (conversation) which takes place in one's thoughts.

(9) INSTINCTS ... are the genetic drives in animal bodies.
(A human spirit does not have instincts). (pages 40, 84-85, 78)

(10) MIND (page 195) ... is our faculty which enables us to react to stimuli in a purposeful manner. This faculty allows us to make judgements, build a value system, make commands for action, and record our doings. The mind is a "doer". It is a builder.

(11) PEACE (page 175) ... is our human sensation of timelessness and eternity.

(12) PURITY (page 173) ... purity is a person's state after removal of any negativity that may be contained in the physical body mind, or in the spirit body and mind.

Practise of the golden light program results in purity.

(13) SELF (pages 15, 101) .. is the repository of one's sense of being an " I am ".

The Self is an harmonic of Basic Energy's force, which individuates everything.

(14) SPIRIT ... the human spirit is a being - which possesses a mind and a body. The core of the spirit is a Self. (page 15)

(15) SYMBIOSIS (page 163) ... is the merger and coordination of a human spirit, into an Homo sapiens body, wherein the spirit remains as a resident.

(16) THOUGHT-FORM (page 145) . . . is an organized body of thought-energy, which contains the directive for this energy to do a specific task.

    (The great pool of golden light is a thought-form, because it contains the unified thought-energy of thousands of Golden persons).

(17) TRUTH (page 185) . . . is only a person's present time sensory information. (Truth is not memory).

ERRATA

My reader should be aware that this book has two definitions for the word <u>enlightened</u> .

My first meaning of enlightened . . . means that one who has become enlightened, is that he or she knows everything ; he or she has infinite knowledge.

Such a person, I believe, cannot exist. This meaning is used by some philosophies and religions.

The second meaning of the word enlightened, as used in this book, is that an enlightened person is wise. He or she knows many things, and is able to have become a Sapere Spiritus. That is, such a person's spirit controls his or her life (and is not controlled by his or her physical body's instincts).

INTRODUCTION

This is about the golden light program – about what it is, and how to practise it and thereby acquire its benefits.

The golden light program is a way of life.

It is somewhat more than a philosophy or religion. Often, those are belief systems that fall short of being the foundation of a life.

The golden light program is of course also a belief system, but must be used, not merely proclaimed.

What is golden light ?

It is the actual light emitted from the spirit bodies of higher type beings.

Such beings are unusual persons, who have the following traits :

(1) they have separated the spirit mind from the physical body mind, and their spirit mind thereupon governs their life ;

(2) they are harmless ;

(3) they love peace, love beauty, love truth, and have compassion for all things and all life.

Those persons who have and live the above traits are called Golden persons (in the terminology of this book).

* * *

The above introduction serves as an outline for this book, and our next chapter will therefore be concerned with the golden light itself.

LIGHT EMISSION

Golden light is emitted from the spirit body of a Golden person.

That light is intense, and makes the aura of a Golden person shining and brilliant.

Question : do less refined persons emit any golden light ?

Yes, they do, but usually, their auras are dominated by another color.

The nature of all persons is revealed by the light that is emitted from the aura.

Light is an energy, a force.

Light is capable of affecting things and conditions.

In the case of a Golden person, his golden light acts to calm, to balance other forces, to reveal the hidden, and to resonate what is held in common.

The golden light of a Golden person is automatically an active force for the improvement and good of all.

LIGHT IS ENERGY

Light is energy.

If anyone doubts this, let him observe how light can be used as a laser to make a hole in steel plate.

Golden light is energy.

And although we have not used it on steel plate, this light affects the forces and conditions of our lives.

Like other energies, which we guide and use to perform work, golden light may also be used.

In fact, it has been doing work for many hundreds of years. And it is active at this very moment.

We have been unaware that golden light constantly acts on our world and on ourselves.

Its nature, to improve anything and everything, wherever improvement is needed . . . is a pressure that slowly and surely elevated humanity.

AUTOMATIC IMPROVEMENT

How is it that anything like a light, can elevate humanity ?

Well - look at sunlight and plants, etc. We couldn't live without that kind of light.

My claim here is that golden light has acted, over centuries, to improve the morals and standards of humanity.

Thus, we have come a long way from the days of "an eye for an eye" and all those super-harsh punishments of old days.

My hypothesis is that in the last six or seven thousand years, there have been thousands of Golden persons evolved out of humanity.

Let us approximate that seven thousand Golden persons now exist in the earth setting, or in a nearby plane of life.

These persons constantly emit golden light from their auras, and do so without intent, as a matter similar to breathing.

Result : a huge pool of golden light now reaches out to the edges of the solar system.

The pool is energy, which contains the thought-force that acts to improve our world.

The force of this pool acts automatically, upon all other forces and conditions of our world.

Golden light requires no direction outside itself.

It acts from its own internal directives.

The pool of golden light became a vast and powerful thought-form.

THE ALLY

A golden light is emitted from the bodies of Golden persons.
That light contains the nature and desires of these persons.

It is not strange or unusual that an emission contains properties of the source of emission.

Almost anything one cares to name, which is an emission, contains properties of its source. This fact is the very foundation, for instance, of work to identify correctly the perpetrator of a crime.

So it is, that thousands of Golden persons, are all of one mind, and emit a golden light which contains their unified desire for improvement and goodness.

That kind of mind-set creates an enormous thought-form.

And it is a thought-form, created by Golden minds, which has been growing larger and more powerful for centuries.

This thought-form may well be the strongest one in existence.

Such a thought-form is a wonderful and dependable ally.
If we have help from this ally, we need have no fears.

I strongly suggest to my readers, think seriously about making this ally your friend.

THE SPECTROSCOPE

Light reveals its source.

We use the spectroscope to analyze the source of light, and determine what chemicals, etc., are present in a light source.

This is done with many kinds of light.

A Golden person, as the source of golden light, is a situation as yet outside the discipline of scientific measurement.

I will therefore propose an hypothesis, about golden light, and its nature.

I propose that : golden light carries the nature and desires of its origin -   and that origin is a Golden person.

Thus, golden light is a force which affects other forces and conditions to improve them.

Improvement is the basic action, because all Golden persons seek the improvement of conditions wherever needed.

The other side of this hypothesis, is that golden light never seeks to act negatively.

It always, like its source, seeks improvement, seeks the positive.

THOUGHT - FORMS

The term "thought-form" was mentioned here - I should define what that term means.

A thought-form is an organized body of thought-energy, which contains the inner directive for this energy to do a specific task.

For example - I create, in my thoughts, the directive in thought-energy, that it bring me a winter coat, which will keep me warm on cold days.

In creating the thought-form, I mentally picture the kind of coat I want, and see myself in it, enjoying warmth.

Then, I "project" the mental energy into the universe.

Next, I wait for the coat to appear.

The body of thought-energy will impinge upon my environment in such a way that the coat I desire will come to me.

The channels taken, for the coat to come to me, will be unknown to me, and not predictable.

This is a simplified version of the thought-form and its workings.

The great golden light thought-form is the product of thousands of minds, all of which have a single and unified view and desire for improvements of humanity.

The golden light thought-form is, of course, far more powerful than that created by a single person.

THE GOLDEN LIGHT POOL

Thousands of Golden persons emit a golden light from their auras, and this is entirely natural.

A Golden person has become governed by his spirit mind, and has thereby become a refined person. This causes his aura to be golden in color, so that it emits golden light.

The golden aura sends out light into the environment.
It is a beacon, a shining light.
And - this light is an energy which carries the nature and desires of the Golden person.
That nature/desire is for the good and improvement of all.

Because thousands of Golden persons exist, their light emission is a great beacon in our solar system.
This huge amount of light forms an enormous "pool".

This pool is a source for power, for those who resonate with golden light.
If you so resonate, you can "plug into" the pool of power.
The pool gives you power, and underwrites your life.

(This is similar to our being able to plug into an electric power grid, and draw power from the grid).

The electric power grid lights our homes.
The golden light power grid lights our lives.

THE AURA

The human aura is generally thought to be merely a light around the body. It is actually much more.

The human aura is our spirit's body.

This was substantiated by Edgar Cayce, who saw a group of people enter an elevator, which broke loose from its cables, fell, and killed all of the occupants. The point here was, that Cayce noticed that none of the occupants had an aura, as they entered the elevator !

The spirits of those entering had left the bodies, somehow knowing that death of the body was imminent.

One can only conclude from this incident, that the aura is the spirit's body.

This will be startling to many of us, because we have not thought of the spirit as possessing a body.

But, a little thought, and we can understand that all entities, of whatever kind, need some kind of body with which to act and be aware of their environment.

Reincarnation is the entry of a spirit-body, into successive lives, of bodies that are Homo sapiens. That entry occurs at birth of the Homo sapiens body.

We can realize from these facts, that the Homo sapiens body, and the spirit body, are both independent entities.

Now, the golden light which we speak so much about herein, is emitted from the spirit body.

The character of one's spirit body determines the color of light, or lights, emitted from it.

An important and primary work for us to do, if we want to achieve a Golden mentality - is to realize that the spirit person, and the Homo sapiens person, are two separate entities.

At present, most of us think these two are the same entity.

In fact, we identify ourselves, almost completely, as the Homo sapiens entity.

The instincts and programs of the Homo sapiens entity govern almost everything we think or do.

The spirit entity, plays little or no role in our lives.

Once we understand that the spirit and physical body are two separate entities, we can begin to allow the spirit to express itself.

In time, the spirit mind should come to govern our lives. That is because the spirit mind is superior to the physical body mind - a spirit mind does not have the burden of instinctive reflex responses, which make too often for irrationality.

This separation of the two minds, is necessary, if one is to achieve the full degree of being Golden.

This separation is explained more extensively in PART TWO of this book.

Illustration -A-, shown on the next and opposing page, is a graphic description of the aura, as it is seen around the Homo sapiens body.

ILLUSTRATION - A -

23'rd PSALM

The pool of golden light acts as a giant thought-form.

This is due to the fact that thousands of Golden persons all feed their thought-energy into a single thought-desire . . . which is for the support and improvement of humanity.

These thoughts and desires of all Golden persons have a perfect unanimity and agreement.

Such unanimity makes for the best kind of thought-form. It contains no contradictions.

And because there are so many (thousands) of Golden persons creating this single, giant thought-form, it is probably one of the most powerful in existence.

This form performs, 24 hours a day, 365 days a year, unceasingly.

As you resonate with golden light and its thought-form, you are helped in every way and endeavor.

For these reasons, I use a part of the 23'd Psalm of the Bible, as an expression of how the golden light works for us.

(In my use of the Psalm, I do not interpret it as a song to a God, but as a description of how golden light is our aid and help).

As follows, here is the part of the Psalm I quote :

" Yea, though I walk through the valley of the shadow of death, I will fear no evil : for thou art with me ; thy rod and thy staff they comfort me ."

PERSONAL THOUGHT-FORMS

The pool of golden light is a giant thought-form. It is composed of the intent and desire of thousands of Golden persons. All of these persons have the same intent and desire (for the good of humanity), so that their thought-energy collectively acts as a single thought-form.

When one becomes a Golden person, he allies himself with the golden light and its giant thought-form.
He thereby receives constant support from the thought-form, which it provides automatically.

A Golden person may also wish to make a personal thought-form.
He may do this, if he so desires.

To make a personal thought-form, the usual technique is followed, with the addition that the visualization (the form) is connected mentally to the pool of golden light.
Visualize the form as flooded with golden light.
The golden light is ultra high energy for the good of all, and will be a force for good in the personal thought-form.

The personal thought-form is projected into the universe when it is completed.
The form contains the power of the golden light, and is thereby far more powerful than ordinary forms.

(A Golden person may discover personal forms are unnecessary. The golden light, as a giant thought-form, often foresees and satisfies problems and needs, before it is necessary to make a personal thought-form).

PART TWO

Separation of the Spirit's Mind From the Physical Body's Mind

A WAY OF LIFE

In the introduction of this book, I said that the golden light program is a way of life.

Which means, the program becomes part of you.

In order to be a Golden person - and be able to benefit fully from all that the golden light can do - the program must become part of you, in many of your daily activities.

The first step in entering the program, is the separation of our two minds.

That is the separation of the spirit mind from the physical body mind.

We humans are two entities, two Selves.

Each Self has a body and its mind.

The minds (not the bodies), can and should be separated.

That separation does not end communication between the spirit and the physical body. Communication continues.

Separation is not easy, because for centuries we have thought of the spirit as being part of the physical body. We did not know that there are two entities involved, and each one is independent.

In our ignorance, we have allowed the physical mind and physical ways and instincts to govern our lives.

To be Golden, we have to learn that the spirit mind must govern us.

Therefore, the first step is - separate the spirit mind from the physical body mind.

How do we do that ?

BEGINNING MIND SEPARATION

Can we separate the spirit mind from the physical body mind ?

Yes, we can -   and one must do it in order to become a Golden person.

It is mandatory to make the separation.

What does separation mean ?

It simply means that the spirit mind knows itself. It becomes fully aware of who and what it is.

At present, in most people, the spirit mind thinks it is the physical body. It identifies with the physical body.

Because the spirit mind does this, it remains unaware of itself as a separate mind from the physical body and physical mind.

* * *

How can we separate our two minds ?

The answer is that one begins by paying extremely close attention to one's "inner dialogue" (which is the talking we all do inside ourselves).

We talk to ourselves most of the time.

So -   try to stand aside from this inner conversation and discover who is talking.

After a time period of listening, one discovers that two entities are present and both talking. Sometimes it is one, and sometimes it is the other.

And each has a character and peculiarities of its own -   which in time help to identify who is talking.

In so listening, one is <u>automatically</u> starting to separate the spirit mind from the physical mind.

Our "inner dialogue" is complex. It requires attentive listening, to separate out the speakers.

That is because two minds are talking, sometimes to each other, and sometimes only to themselves.
We have a mult-layered dialogue.

The spirit's mind will talk to itself.
Or, it will talk to the physical body's mind.

The same thing is true for the physical body's mind.
It talks to itself, and also talks to the spirit's mind.

(You can see how complicated this can become).

NOTE : these two minds do the talking.
That is to say, the Self of the spirit, and the Self of the physical body, do not talk -   nor do they make judgements and command actions.
A Self is only the sense of being an "I am", a sensation which creates the awareness that an individual is only itself, and not those things which surround it.

The mind of the spirit, and the mind of the physical body are each able to build a value system.
At present, our spirit minds have mimed, or copied the value system built by the physical body.
As the value systems contact sensations, we respond with our associations, evaluations, and talking.

As we practise intense listening, we wait and monitor this talking.

INTENSE LISTENING

The first step to separate the spirit mind from the physical body mind is to listen intensely to our inner dialogue.

We have a faculty, which enables us to stand aside and listen to the dialogue, as if we were outside ourselves, listening.

That faculty is the property of a Self, and is in the spirit Self, and also in the physical body Self.

Thus, a Self has an "observer" faculty.

This is the act of observing, without making any comment, or doing something in response to what is observed.

The part of a being which commands action, and is a "doer", is the mind of that being.

The mind of any being builds a value system, talks, and commands what actions it deems required.

A Self is not a doer. It is an observer, but not an actor.

As we learn to listen to inner dialogue, the Self of the spirit, and the Self of the physical body, are observers.

Listen intently, and discover who is talking.

This listening automatically begins the separation of the minds.

SEPARATION MANDATORY

We are able to separate the spirit mind from the physical body mind. This is mandatory.

(It does not mean the two minds cease communication. The minds do continue to communicate).

This separation allows the spirit mind to stop thinking it is a physical body -   and allows the spirit mind to become aware of itself, and know who and what it is.

Why mandatory ?
Separation is mandatory if we want to become a Golden person.

If we do not so separate, we remain in thrall to the physical body, which is an animal that responds reflexively to its instincts.
This animal, the Homo sapiens, is very short on being rational, and long on emotion and violence.
(At this moment, armies gather again).

The Golden person is governed by his spirit mind.
He is not violent.
To remain in thrall to physical instinct, defeats the work we must do to become a Golden person.

SYMBIOSIS

Why do our spirits think that they are the physical body ?
Answer : it is a matter of symbiosis.

Our spirit bodies merge into the primate body, at birth of the infant.
This begins a symbiotic relationship between body and spirit.
(Let us remember, the spirit and body both remain independent, and each has its own life force. The physical body is not dependent upon the spirit for life).

Upon merging into the infant's body (which is a primate animal), the spirit is forced to partake of the infant's inabilities.
The spirit then goes into a non-active period, and doesn't express itself until the infant becomes a small child.
When the infant grows into a small child, the spirit usually begins to express itself. Sometimes, the spirit talks of its previous life in another primate body. Small children are noted for doing this.

As the small child matures, the spirit becomes more and more locked into an identification with and as the child's physical body.
The spirit uses the muscles, nerves, brain, etc., increasingly - and becomes so habituated to this use, that the spirit deepens its feeling that it is the physical body being used.

By the age of six or seven, almost everyone's spirit feels it is the physical body.

This is the mistake we must correct, if we are to become Golden.

-163-

CHEATING YOURSELF

In nearly everyone, the spirit mind is not separated from the physical body mind. And as said, this is a mistake that cheats people out of their becoming Golden persons.

Instead, people go through many lives over the centuries, and continue to be ruled by emotion and violence.

Our human history is very, very bloody.

If the two minds are not separated, the spirit continues to think it is a primate, and acts accordingly.

If the spirit mind thinks it is a primate, it does not resonate with golden light.

The principles of golden light, and the forces of primate instinct, oppose each other.

A primate mind does not (and probably cannot), understand or agree with genuine peacefulness ; its idea of beauty is skewed toward sex ; its truthfulness is corrupted by self-serving and pleasure ; and its compassion is not universal.

If a person remains primate-minded, he remains not a candidate for becoming a Golden person.

He is cheating himself.

WHY SEPARATION ?

Why is it mandatory to separate the spirit mind from the physical body mind   -   if we want to be a Golden person ?

As remarked, if we remain physical-minded (ruled by physical desires and instincts), we will remain ruled by some degree of violence.
We are then unable to love genuine peace.

And as well, when ruled by physicality, we are basically unable to love real beauty, truth, and compassion.

If one is ruled by physicality, he does not resonate with or care for the golden light program.

But   -   when the spirit mind is separated from the physical mind, the spirit mind can then recall its original state.
Which was   -   a state of non-violence.
The spirit was originally peaceful and childlike.
Thus, an independent spirit mind is able to resonate with the golden light program, quite naturally.

Once we achieve separation, we can become candidates for the golden light program.
But first, we need to learn of that program, study it, practise it, and go on to become our best   -   a Golden person.

OTHER MEANS OF SEPARATION

Careful listening to one's inner dialogue was given as a means to separate the spirit mind from the physical body mind.

This listening, by the Selves, is a good way to observe the two minds in action. Listening gives us a way to separate these minds.

There are other means to help separate the minds. Let me name some.

Out of body experiences :

some people have out of body experiences. If you have these, you have no doubt that a spirit body exists, and has a mind of its own.

That knowledge helps you to separate the two minds. It is easier for you to become governed by a spirit mind that no longer thinks it is the physical body.

Daily life observations :

if you watch your physical body mind seek pleasure, security, and so forth -   you learn the actuality of how the physical mind works.

You can then notice how occasionally a different sort of mind enters into your thinking, and you discover the spirit mind. You see the difference between the two minds.

You learn the reality of the spirit mind.

General studies :

one can study the mind problem in a general manner. Reading, talking to other persons, etc., leads us to make general and theoretical ideas about the two minds.

From general studies, we can begin to make "hands on" testing.

The goal remains, no matter how we approach it.
Separate the two minds, and release the spirit mind from its bondage.

PART THREE

Practice of the Golden Light Program

A GOLDEN PERSON IS ENLIGHTENED

The first parts of this book have accented that we must separate the spirit mind from the physical body mind.

Then, the spirit mind can discover it is not the physical body.

(Most people feel that their spirit is the physical body).

This basic mistake needs correction.

To practise the golden light program, we must free ourselves from the mistaken idea that our spirit is the physical body and its mind.

If we do not free ourselves, the practices of peace, beauty, truth, and compassion -   become distorted.

When we free the spirit mind to return to its original nature, which is one of peacefulness, we can practise peace, beauty, etc., correctly.

The proper practise of the golden light program leads one into the state of enlightenment.

In that state, one resonates with golden light and enjoys its benefits, and is aware of his oneness with the universe.

To be enlightened, you genuinely love peace, love beauty, love truth, and have compassion for all life.

In the state of enlightenment, you are master of the physical body's programs.

This does not mean that you mistreat the physical body in any way.

On the contrary, the physical body is well cared for (it is treated as one treats a beloved pet).

The following chapters will discuss the golden light program.

PURIFICATION

What does it mean to "practise" the golden light program ?

It means that you live in such a way that your thoughts and actions purify and refine you.

When purity becomes your condition, you resonate with other Golden persons, and with the golden light they emit.

You, too, emit golden light, and add to the great pool of this light.

You become a good, for everyone and everything.

Purity means, that you have removed negativity from your physical body, and from your spirit body. And as well, the minds of these bodies have been purified and refined.

The total frequency of your symbiotic relationship, has been made a new state.

Purification and refinement are a restructuring of one's neural patterns in the physical body - and a renewal of one's original innocence, of his spirit's personality.

This restructuring and renewal result in a new kind of symbiotic being. He is a Golden person. His overall combination of frequencies produces golden light from him.

True purification is not done to you or for you.
You must do it for yourself.

PEACE

The first work in the golden light program, is the separation of the spirit mind from the physical body's mind. The spirit mind must come to understand that it is not the physical body.

As this work continues, the spirit mind comes to know itself, and it ceases to identify itself as the physical body.

At the same time, the spirit mind slowly begins to recall its original nature, which was one of peacefulness and innocence.

It knew no hostility, violence, or deceit.

Over time, the spirit mind then makes a slow return to its original nature.

When this return is near its completion, the spirit is able to govern the physical body's mind and instincts.

Physical impulses to have and hold territory, to have sex and procreate, and to be social with leaders and leadership - all will become controlled and tethered.

Peace controls violence.

Instinct contains latent violence.

The spirit originally knew or contained no violence.

The renewed and recalled spirit is a lover of peace, and casts out all violence.

Instinct is controlled and tethered.

* * *

The human spirit is able to observe and delight in the soft flow of seasons, of years that pass, and the sense of space in endless time.

The incidents of the moment, some important and some not - are imbued by peace with timelessness.

Stress vanishes.

Delight in the time-flow, replaces stress.

Peace casts out stress.

Peace has a sensation of eternity.

* * *

The Golden person emits peace from himself (other people often remark about his peaceful nature).

He soothes, comforts, and heals. He builds loving relationships.

His golden light creates peace around him.

CORRECTION

In the previous words about "Peace" -   I have possibly given a wrong impression.

That is, I said the spirit mind returns to its original nature, of being peaceful and innocent.

This is true, however, I do not want to create the idea that the spirit forgets all it has experienced and learned, while it thought that it was the physical body.

Nothing is forgotten.

The spirit remembers intimately, its subservience to the primate ways and instincts.

The matured and freed spirit understands what it has been through.

And the freed spirit can now use that information to judge what the world is doing.

(The freed spirit can now "see through" the clever deceits of those around him).

The freed spirit, the Golden person, may be peaceful and innocent, but he has a wise innocence.

The Golden person lives in the world, but is not of the world.

He is not of the world, but is completely wise to the ways of the world.

FOUR MAGIC WORDS

Peace, beauty, truth, and compassion are practised by the Golden person.

He embodies these traits.

(I often call these four traits, by the term "Four Magic Words").

When we have succeeded, at least partially, to separate the spirit mind from its belief it is the physical body, the spirit then begins to know and exert its true nature. It sees that its nature is quite different from that of the physical body/mind.

In fact, the spirit discovers how its true nature harmonizes with the four magic words.

With this discovery, the spirit has made its beginning in the golden light program.

* * *

Upon entry into the golden light program, the spirit may become more peaceful - or it may put more attention into one or more of the other four magic words.

A person may, for example, start doing some form of art, in response to his attention upon beauty.

At the same time, former physical body ways and instincts begin to hold less appeal.

Much less appeal.

As time passes, physical body ways and instincts will become fully under control. They become "tethered".

Becoming a Golden person takes time. For some, a relatively short time - for most, rather a long time.

We have spent many lives thinking we are a physical body. It has become a deeply strong habit.

All world cultures base their beliefs and practises upon the belief that we are the physical body. Homo sapiens rules.

Be patient with yourself.

The belief that you are the physical body will overturn the spirit's decisions, time after time.

The trip along the road of the golden light program is demanding.

And it is well to remember, on this trip, that it will be all your own efforts.

You are the only person who can make you into a Golden person.

BEAUTY

The second of the four magic words is beauty.

A Golden person embodies the four words (traits), which describe his life. He lives the words, and they work their magic, to purify him.

He becomes Golden, and radiates golden light.

The golden light carries in it the nature of those who radiate it. Thus, this light acts to purify, to heal the world.

This is a large claim, but truthful.

The first of the four magic words was peace, which casts out stress. Peace allows our human view of timelessness and eternity.

Peace gives us the "long view" of ourselves and our doings.

The second of the four words is beauty.

What is beauty ?

(We hear so many opinions).

The definition used in this book, is that beauty is <u>whatever</u> is balanced and harmonious.

Actions, things, concepts, scenes, etc. - can all be beautiful.

The key words to describe beauty, are balance and harmony.

* * *

Both spirit mind and physical body mind, are able to respond to their perceptions of balance and harmony.

But - we need to use care in this, because, our physical mind often confuses sex with beauty.

(Young, smooth women are called beautiful ; whereas, that is sexual response, not a response to balance and harmony).

As we work with the golden light program, we will give attention to those things that are balanced and harmonious.

Enjoy and dwell on these experiences.

One should also think thoughts, and perform actions, in ways that are balanced and harmonious.

Our activities with beauty may take all manner of ways and byways. The student in the golden light program, must invent these ways and byways for himself. He must do for himself, and make the golden light program "his".

He is a self-starter.

He finds his own personal ways to beauty.

* * *

The golden light program, using the four magic words, helps us to return our spirit-self to its full self-knowledge and awareness.

ABSTRACTIONS

Yes -   of course the four magic words are abstractions.
That is, they remain only words, until they become experience.

When the four words are put into action, they cease to be abstractions and become the reality of sensation.

This is an important juncture.
The juncture is that time and place, whereat the student of golden light goes beyond the word, the abstraction, and goes into the experience of beauty, or peace, or truth, or compassion.

So often, people live by words alone, and believe they know the reality of what is happening.
For the most part, they do not know.
Words mislead, when they are the sole content of one's thought.

We do well to get the sensation, the reality, <u>first.</u>
And then, we can allow ourselves the luxury of words to describe the sensation.

This concept is so important, that some wise persons, have even made themselves stop talking entirely.
They were intent upon staying in direct contact with sensation, with their reality.
We don't have to stop talking entirely, but let us be careful how we remain close to reality, and suspicious of words.

The next chapter is about truth, the third of the magic words.
Truth -   is our reality, our sensations.
Let us remember, sensations are what we <u>really</u> have.

TRUTH

The golden light program uses the Four Magic Words as guides to our behavior.

We come now to the third word, which is truth.

There are many definitions of truth, or reality, and I will define it as follows, for the purposes of the program.

Truth (reality) is only each person's sensory information, received in present time.

Note : memory is not defined as truth.

This is the case, because memory is always diluted and modified. It is no longer the fresh sensation of the moment.

To know truth, we have to be careful not to allow memory to intrude upon and change the sense information of the present moment.

As we accept that our memories are not truth, we allow ourselves to be more careful about how much we trust memory.

The great bulk of memory is what our culture believes and teaches us, from childhood and on. And most of that is false.

In order to become Golden, one must remain fully rational and truthful.

Be as logical and scientific as possible.

And remember, that even the truth of our present time sensation, will give us but a small amount of what really is.

TRUTH REVIEW

The golden light program student, must examine his memories.

Study your memories -   all those things the culture has put into your mind.

The unconscious level of mind is filled with the culture's teachings and beliefs.

The culture's hand is on your every thought.

And much of what the culture has given you is false.

The base of all cultures, contains an enormous amount of falsehood.

Which -   determines how people think, and what are their values.

The enlightened Golden person reviews and "sees through", the material that runs this world.

Study truth, and become skilled in separating present time sense information from recalled memory.

Skill in knowing truth, is the foundation of being Golden.

COMPASSION

The last of the Four Magic Words is compassion.

Compassion is ... for other people, and everything else.

It is sympathy, mercy, tenderness, and a sharing of what others have to endure.

If I am compassionate toward another person, I do not berate, ridicule, punish, etc., for his shortcomings and misfortune.

A Golden person is a deep well of sympathy and understanding.

This is a well of living water.

* * *

Note : compassion is different from love.

The difference is that love involves an exchange of real energy between persons. The real energy is absorbed into the bodies of those who are involved.

The energy remains in their bodies.

With compassion, no energy is exchanged. Often, the subjects of compassion are not known to the giver of compassion.

In a world filled with endless conflict, compassion is a sorely needed thing.

The Golden person provides this precious thing.

SUMMARY

Why should anyone want to become a Golden person ?

The answer is simple. When you become a Golden person, you have attained the best you can be.

The Golden person is top level attainment for the human being.

The first step of that attainment is separation of the spirit mind from the Homo sapiens mind.

The human spirit rediscovers itself.

It stops believing it is the physical body.

This rediscovery is mandatory.

It is mandatory, because if you continue to think you are the physical body, you remain in thrall to its demands.

And those demands, instincts, contain latent or expressed violence, and that violence opposes the peacefulness of the spirit mind.

Physical instinct blocks spirit rediscovery.

As long as a person remains in thrall to instinct, he will discover no spirituality.

He may, yes, discover substitutes and imitations of spirituality.

* * *

Let us assume you begin to separate the spirit mind from the mind of the physical body.

Slowly, the spirit mind stops believing it is the physical body.

Two Selves now become apparent.

They are the Self of the spirit, and the Self of the physical body.

And as well, two minds become apparent - the mind of the spirit, and also the mind of the physical body.

As you listen to your inner dialogue, the two Selves observe and hear the two minds converse. The minds talk to each other, and to themselves all the time.

This creates a complex dialogue.

Persistent observation of your inner dialogue automatically begins the separation of spirit mind from the physical body's mind.

* * *

Finally, as you feel aware of being a spirit, you are ready to begin a genuine practise of the four magic words.

The words are : peace, beauty, truth, and compassion.

This practise is central to all you think or do.

These words slowly form a new value system for both the spirit mind and the physical body mind.

You are now embarked upon your great work to become a Golden person.

PART FOUR

BASIC ENERGY

Basic Energy is the "stuff" from which the universe is made.
This energy is the common denominator of everything.

In Basic Energy, two processes are always at work. The processes are creation, and destruction.

Hindu cosmology calls Basic Energy by the name of Brahma.
Creative forces are named Vishnu.
The destructive forces are named Siva.

Interestingly, Hindu cosmology contains the idea that once in a great while, the Siva forces destroy everything -   which marks the end of a time period called a Kalpa.
A new Kalpa is then begun, as the Vishnu forces create another and new universe.

* * *

One of the works of Vishnu forces is to individualize everything.
In our human instance, this individuation is seen as our Self.
The Self is the repository of our sense of being an "I am". The Self is an harmonic of a real force, and thus, the Self is a real thing.

The spirit is a body and a Self.
Likewise, the physical body is body and Self.

Some people believe the human spirit and Self are immortal.
This belief would seem to place the human spirit outside the powers of Siva, the destroyer.
We are unable to know, ever, if this belief contains any truth.

MIND

As far as we can ascertain, most beings develope some kind of mind.

And essentially, a mind is the ability to react in a purposeful manner to stimuli.

The Homo sapiens type of mind has levels. These levels are called the unconscious, the subconscious, and the conscious. Each level reacts in its own ways to stimuli.

The Homo sapiens mind builds a value system, which is a set of guides for behavior.

Unfortunately, our spirit's mind mimes the Homo sapiens' value system and this act by the spirit mind makes it hard to differentiate the spirit mind from the physical body mind.

Thus, most of us are unaware we are spirits.

The usual value system is flawed by the many falsehoods, taught us by our culture. Our value systems need to be cleansed.

As one practises the "four magic words", his value system becomes purified. That is to say, the falsehoods taught by the culture are exposed and eliminated.

This purification takes place, both in the spirit mind and in the mind of the physical body.

Purification of the value system aids and encourages our becoming a Golden person.

BENEFITS

What is the advantage of being a Golden person ?

The advantage is, that a Golden person enjoys many and constant benefits, because he is Golden.

For instance, a Golden person is protected from harm at all times.

He is protected from any kind of harm.

The great golden light thoughtform will foresee the approach of harm to a Golden person, and will repel the harm.

Golden light provides a shield.

The golden light will bring to him, needed information.

The golden light thoughtform does not have to be asked for the needed information. The information is brought automatically.

For the Golden person, golden light will assist him in productions.

For example, if the Golden person is painting a picture, the golden light will bring items, ideas, etc., that assist the painting.

This will be true for any productive work.

Exposure of other persons - the mental status of people near the Golden person, or anyone who can affect his activities - will be made known.

The Golden person will be led into the life environment that is best suited to him.

The Golden person reaps these and other benefits. In addition, he has complete peace in himself, and does good for all.

His cup truly runs over.

RELIGION

The golden light program is not a religion.
It is a way of life.
One might call the program a living philosophy.

The program does not advocate worship of, or praying to, a God, or to Gods.

Nor does the program advocate following rules that are claimed to be given by a God or Gods.

The questions about a supreme being, or beings, is left to the decisions of the participant in the golden light program.

It should be noted, however, that a Golden person lives a life that is considered proper and desirable, by almost all religions.

THE WORLD

A Golden person lives in the world, but is not of the world.

This means, a Golden person is not controlled by his physical body instincts. Instead, his spirit mind controls his life.

This control is the major difference between the person of the world, and the Golden person.

The people of the world are controlled by their physical body instincts.

They have not discovered that they are spirits, but continue to think they are the physical body.

If anyone thinks he is the physical body, it will control what he does and what he thinks.

Because all the world thinks it is the physical body, every culture and its people are acting out whatever the instincts of the physical body have been evolved to produce.

Thus, if you are controlled by instinct, you quite naturally become part of the world's many conflicts.

You "take sides", and struggle against the opposition, whatever it might be.

The Golden person finds that he cannot take the world's conflicts to be his own.

He is not a part of any conflicts.

From his view, all sides of conflicts, are in the wrong.

That is because, instinct and its violence are the basics of every side of every conflict.

All sides are violent,

All sides of any confict are wrong.

* * *

Thus, the Golden person finds very few kindred spirits.

He is a "loner".

But, he is free from conflict, while everyone else is embroiled in some area or kind of conflict.

The Golden person is free from instinct - while at the same time, he takes good care of the physical body and regards it as a pet.

He is non-animal.

Physical body instinct is pure animal, and those who are in servitude to it, are forced to be animalistic.

Animal instinct contains latent violence, and this often becomes the outward thing, real and expressed violence.

All of that, lacks balance and harmony.

It is well nigh impossible, for those who are animalistic, to practise peace, beauty, truth, and compassion.

* * *

Would you be a Golden person ?

Then - expect to be apart from this world.

The world has always been, and remains, animal.

The Golden person is the next higher level of spiritual evolution.

"Look homeward, Angel."

www.ingramcontent.com/pod-product-compliance
Lightning Source LLC
Chambersburg PA
CBHW082115230426
43671CB00015B/2707